DIRECTIONS IN DEVELOPMENT

Environmental Health and Traditional Fuel Use in Guatemala

RENEWALS 458-4574

DATE DUE

DIRECTIONS IN DEVELOPMENT

Environmental Health and Traditional Fuel Use in Guatemala

Kulsum Ahmed, Yewande Awe, Douglas F. Barnes,
Maureen L. Cropper, and Masami Kojima

ESMAP (Energy Sector Management Assistance Program)

THE WORLD BANK
Washington, D.C.

Cover: The image of the woman was purchased in Guatemala City at the Mercado Central en Guatemala, where handicrafts of Chinautla, Coban, Quetzaltenango, and other areas are available. Artist unknown.

ISBN 0-8213-6082-5
e-ISBN 0-8213-6083-3

Library of Congress Cataloging-in-Publication Data has been applied for.

Table of Contents

Acknowledgments viii

Abbreviations and Acronyms x

Units of Measure xii

Executive Summary xiii

1. Introduction 1

2. Indoor Air Pollution and Health: Evidence from
   the Demographic and Health Survey and the
   Living Standards Measurement Study 11

3. Estimating Health Impacts 28

4. The Evolution of Improved Stoves in Guatemala:
   Lessons from Three Programs 49

5. The Role of LPG 81

6. Policy Recommendations 93

Bibliography 104

Index...110

Tables
1.1 Five Principal Causes of General Morbidity and Five
    Principal Causes of Mortality in Guatemala, 1997–2000 3
1.2 Comparison of Indoor Pollution Levels from Open Fire,
    Plancha, and LPG Stove in the Guatemalan Highlands.............. 6
2.1 Sample Distribution: Guatemala 1998–1999 DHS 13
2.2 Sample Distribution: Guatemala 2000 LSMS 15

2.3 Guatemalan Households with Electricity 17
2.4 Distribution of Main or Single Fuels Used for Cooking
    in Guatemala from 1998–1999 DHS 18
2.5 Summary of All Fuels Used for Cooking by Guatemalan
    Households 20
2.6 Combination of Fuels and Kitchen Facilities in
    Guatemalan Homes 22
2.7 Respiratory Symptoms in Children by Fuel and Cooking
    Space from 1998–1999 DHS 24
2.8 Respiratory Symptoms in Children by Fuel and Cooking
    Space from 2000 LSMS 25
3.1 Percentage of Rural Households Using Fuelwood,
    Conditional on House Characteristics 31
3.2 Personal and Daily Average Kitchen Measurements of
    Particulate Matter in the Guatemalan Highlands 33
3.3 Adjusted Odds Ratios for ARI and ALRI in Children
    under Age Five Estimated with a Logistic Model 36
3.4 Excess Cases of ALRI Morbidity and Mortality in
    the Guatemalan Highlands Associated with IAP 38
3.5 Number of Children under Age Five and ALRI
    Incidence Rates 39
3A.1 Biomass Fuel Use and ALRI in Children under
    Age Five in Developing Countries 42
4.1 Stages in the Development of Stove Technology 51
4.2 Communities Selected for the Study 56
4.3 Typical Subsidies of Three Programs in
    Rural Guatemala, 2002 64
4.4 Comparisons of Stove Issues for Six Villages in
    Three Improved Stove Projects 67
4.5 Problems with Improved Stove Chimneys in
    Guatemala, 2002 68
4.6 The Benefits of Improved Stoves in Two Programs
    in Guatemala, 2002 69
4.7 Positive Aspects of the Improved Stoves
    Project Case Studies 73
4.8 Weaknesses of the Improved Stoves
    Project Case Studies 75
5.1 Household Fuel Use Patterns for Cooking and Heating 82
5.2 LPG Availability and Uptake by Households 83
5.3 Cylinder Sizes in Guatemala 84
5.4 Retail Cost of LPG Cylinder and Stove 85
5.5 Mean Monthly per Capita and Household Expenditures 85
5.6 Retail Prices of LPG Sold in 25 lb (11.4 kg) Cylinders,
    April 22–28, 2002 86

Figures

1.1 Energy Options, Ranked by Increasing Effectiveness
     in Mitigating the Health Impacts of IAP 2
4.1 Typical Plancha Stove Promoted by the Social Fund
     in Guatemala 54
4.2 The Tezulutlán Stove 59
4.3 Varieties of Intervida-Type Stove 60
4.4 Stoves in Rural Households 62
4.5 Firebox Differences between Stoves.. 65
5.1 Comparison of LPG Prices (exclusive of taxes)................................ 88
5.2 Price of LPG Sold in 25 lb (11.4 kg) Cylinder in
     Guatemala City 89

Acknowledgments

This study was undertaken by the Latin America and Caribbean Regional Office of the World Bank as a joint effort between the Energy and Environment Units, in close coordination with the Health Unit and with support from ESMAP (Energy Sector Management Assistance Program). The financial assistance of the governments of the Netherlands and Germany is gratefully acknowledged.

The report responds to a request from the Ministry of Energy and Mines (MEM) in Guatemala to seek a better understanding of the implications of indoor air pollution in Guatemala and of the corresponding mitigation options. Special gratitude is extended to MEM Vice Minister Santizo for his personal interest and leadership in this area, and to Milton Saravia, MEM Environment Unit Coordinator and direct counterpart for this study.

Particular mention should also be made of the multisectoral participants who attended the two dissemination workshops in Guatemala held in November 2001 and April 2003. These participants represented a wide spectrum of Guatemalan sectors and stakeholders, including the government of Guatemala (the Ministry of Energy and Mines, the Ministry of Health, the Ministry of Environment and Natural Resources, and the Social Investment Fund), academia, the private sector, and nongovernmental organizations. These participants provided guidance to the Bank team, helping us to ground our recommendations in the reality of the Guatemalan context. They are the champions of this cause, as Guatemala moves forward to address the issues that are so closely linked with its development priorities.

This report is based on the work of several consultants: José Eddy Torres (survey analysis); Fundación Solar (improved stoves), including Iván Azurdia-Bravo, Manuel Tay, Danilo Álvarez, and Carolina Palma; Rogério Carneiro de Miranda (improved stoves); William Matthews (LPG); and Alejandra Palma (health impacts).

The core World Bank team for this study includes Kulsum Ahmed (Task Team Leader), Yewande Awe (Co-Task Team Leader), Douglas

Barnes (improved stoves and survey analysis), Katia Nemes (Workshop Coordinator), Masami Kojima (LPG component), and Maureen Cropper (health impacts component). Peer reviewers include Kseniya Lvovsky (Lead Environment Economist) and Marcelo Bortman (Public Health Specialist). Report formatting assistance was provided by Erica Felix. In addition, the team would particularly like to acknowledge the support and close involvement, during the course of this activity and the subsequent preparation of this report, of Susan Goldmark (Latin America and the Caribbean Region Energy Sector Manager); Dominique Lallement (Manager, Energy Sector Management Assistance Program [ESMAP]); Marjorie K. Araya (ESMAP) who coordinated production, printing, and dissemination in conjunction with Office of the Publisher staff; Eduardo Somensatto (Guatemala Country Manager); and Helena Ribe (Health Sector Leader for Central America). The Sector Manager for this activity was Susan Goldmark (Latin America and the Caribbean Region, Energy Cluster); the Finance, Public Sector and Infrastructure (FPSI) Sector Leader was Manuel Sevilla (LCC2C); the FPSI Sector Director was Danny Leipziger; the Central America Country Director was Jane Armitage; and the Latin America and the Caribbean Regional Vice President was David de Ferranti.

Abbreviations and Acronyms

ALRI	acute lower respiratory infection
ARI	acute respiratory infection
AURI	acute upper respiratory tract infection
CI	confidence interval
CO	carbon monoxide
COGUANOR	Comisión Guatemalteca de Normas (Guatemalan Commission for Standards)
COPD	chronic obstructive pulmonary disease
DALY	disability-adjusted life year
DGH	Dirección General de Hidrocarburos (General Directorate of Hydrocarbons)
DHS	Demographic and Health Survey
ENCOVI	Encuesta Nacional sobre Condiciones de Vida (Living Standards Measurement Study)
ENSMI	Encuesta Nacional de Salud Materno Infantil (Demographic Health Survey)
ESMAP	Energy Sector Management Assistance Program
ETS	environmental tobacco smoke
FIS	Fondo de Inversión Social (Social Investment Fund)
GDP	gross domestic product
HSE	health, safety, and environment
IAP	indoor air pollution
LPG	liquefied petroleum gas
LSMS	Living Standards Measurement Study
MDG	Millennium Development Goal
MEM	Ministerio de Energía y Minas (Ministry of Energy and Mines)
MSPAS	Ministerio de Salud Publica y Asistencia Social (Ministry of Public Health and Social Assistance)
NGO	nongovernmental organization
PM	particulate matter

PM_{10}	particles with an aerodynamic diameter less than 10 microns
$PM_{2.5}$	particles with an aerodynamic diameter less than 2.5 microns
$PM_{3.5}$	particles with an aerodynamic diameter less than 3.5 microns
TSP	total suspended particles
UNDP	United Nations Development Programme
WHO	World Health Organization

Units of Measure

g/m³	grams per cubic meter
lb	pound (454 grams)
mg/m³	milligrams per cubic meter
mm	millimeter
ppm	parts per million
Q.	(Guatemalan) Quetzal
μg/m³	micrograms per cubic meter
μm	micron (one-thousandth of a millimeter)

Executive Summary

Recognition of the problem of indoor air pollution (IAP) and its harmful effects on health is growing worldwide as efforts increase to understand and articulate the complex health–air pollution links. Half the world's population is exposed to IAP, mainly from burning solid fuels for cooking and heating. A recent World Health Organization (WHO) report concluded that consistent evidence exists that exposure to biomass smoke increases the risk of a range of common and serious diseases in both children and adults (WHO 2002). Most notable among these diseases are acute lower respiratory infections (ALRIs)[1] in childhood, in particular, pneumonia. The report also identified IAP from solid fuels as one of the 10 leading risk factors responsible for a substantial proportion of the leading causes of death and disability. Indoor smoke from solid fuels causes an estimated 1.6 million deaths annually and accounts for 2.7 percent of the global burden of disease.

The literature and experience from various countries indicate that mitigation of the health impacts of IAP can be achieved as households move up the energy ladder, from wood to cleaner liquid or gaseous fuels such as kerosene and liquefied petroleum gas (LPG), and ultimately to electricity. At the lower end of the energy ladder, better ventilation and the use of improved biomass stoves that vent smoke through a chimney and away from the cooking area can decrease exposure to emissions of harmful pollutants. Policy options that would facilitate the penetration of these improvements are cross-sectoral and include fuel pricing and distribution policies, small business development, income generation activities, and health education. Behavioral and cultural factors are important when considering the technical mitigation options and, along with lack of information, often are the greater barriers that need to be addressed to achieve positive health effects.

Nature of the Problem in Guatemala

Recent statistics from the Ministerio de Salud Publica y Asistencia Social (MSPAS) in Guatemala indicate that between 1997 and 2000 acute respiratory infection (ARI) was the single most important cause of morbidity and mortality in Guatemala.[2] In this period, the number of cases of morbidity due to ARI grew by an average of 31 percent per year.[3] In the same period, ARI caused on average two to three times as many deaths as acute diarrhea, the second most important cause of mortality in Guatemala. As a subset of these data, the impact of ARI on the health of children in Guatemala is particularly important. In 1997–2000, pneumonia represented the most important single cause of infant death in Guatemala. In 2000, it accounted for 36 percent of all registered deaths among infants.

IAP in Guatemala is closely linked with the following:

- *High incidence of poverty.* More than half of all Guatemalans (56 percent, or about 6.4 million people) were living in poverty in 2000.
- *Low levels of rural electrification.* Fewer than 40 percent of the poorest households have electricity connections, compared to 95 percent of the richest households.
- *Large rural population.* More than 60 percent of the Guatemalan population lives in rural areas, including 81 percent of the poor and 93 percent of the extreme poor. Three-quarters of all rural residents fall below the full poverty line, and one-quarter live in extreme poverty.
- *High levels of traditional fuel use.* Fuelwood is the dominant cooking fuel in 97 percent of households in rural areas. Among rural households, 42 percent use fuelwood only and 55 percent use wood and one or more other fuels.

Context for This Report

This report represents the final activity in a series of projects that have focused on the problem of IAP and its impacts on health in rural households in Guatemala. The study was carried out between October 2001 and June 2003, with support from ESMAP (Energy Sector Management Assistance Program). This report summarizes the findings of each of a series of substudies, as well as two workshops, and presents final recommendations.

The objectives of this study were to estimate the health impacts of traditional fuel use and to outline strategies and policies for mitigating environmental health damage due to household energy. Mitigation of IAP from the use of traditional biomass fuels is identified as a high priority in the World Bank's *Fuel for Thought: Environmental Strategy for the Energy Sector* (World Bank 1999). Given the close link between IAP and women's and children's health, this study additionally provides information for the government with respect to achievement of the Millennium Development Goals (MDGs) of reducing child mortality and improving maternal health.

The major activities carried out under the study included individual studies of specific aspects of the IAP and health matrix, as well as two dissemination workshops. The specific studies carried out under the overall study are listed below and are described in more detail in the body of the report:

- a review of the existing literature on IAP and health globally and in Guatemala, and an estimate of the health implications of failure to address the problem of ARI and IAP either through policy interventions or technical mitigation measures
- a review of two major surveys conducted in Guatemala—the 1998–99 Demographic and Health Survey (DHS) (or *Encuesta Nacional de Salud Materno Infantil* 1998–99, ENSMI) and the 2000 National Living Standards Measurement Study (LSMS) (or *Encuesta Nacional sobre Condiciones de Vida* 2000, ENCOVI)—to investigate potential relationships between energy use and IAP
- an evaluation of improved stoves programs in Guatemala and a focused review of the cost structure of stoves under such programs
- a study of the LPG industry and market in Guatemala

These activities were chosen to specifically complement existing activities under way in Guatemala at the time, including a Poverty Assessment, financed by the Bank; an ESMAP-sponsored network in Central America on Women and Improved Stoves; and exposure monitoring through an intervention study financed by the U.S. National Institutes of Health. In addition, at the time of the study the Bank and other development partners were providing support to the Guatemalan Social Investment Fund (Fondo de Inversion Social, FIS). The work of the FIS included, as one component in a menu of poverty reduction actions, the largest improved stoves program in Guatemala. A particular focus of this study was a review of this program and the formulation of policy recommendations to enhance its impact in the effort to reduce IAP.

Link with Millennium Development Goals

A growing body of evidence, based on worldwide IAP health studies, indicates that the levels of IAP in homes that use traditional solid fuels are alarmingly high. Exposure monitoring studies in Guatemala confirmed that women and children endure high exposure to toxic pollutants from fuelwood consumption. The worldwide literature also points to a strong association between IAP and health conditions, particularly among children in the first few years of life. Conclusive links between health and IAP are still lacking, but a recently initiated study in the Guatemalan highlands, financed by the U.S. National Institutes of Health, is expected to be an important source of information.

Informal estimates, however, based on the results of worldwide IAP health studies, indicate that the number of annual cases of ALRI in the Guatemalan highlands could be reduced by as many as 24,000, and annual deaths by about 1,000, through the elimination of indoor air pollution. This would be about a 60 percent reduction in the annual cases of ALRI mortality among the 400,000 children under age five who live in households in which open fires are used for cooking.

Despite the lack of conclusive evidence on the extent of health impacts, the general consensus among the broad range of Guatemalan stakeholders represented at the April 2003 workshop was that something has to be done about the problem in the short term. This consensus was reinforced by the problem's close link with the fourth MDG, related to reducing child mortality, and with the fifth MDG, related to improving maternal health. This consensus is also consistent with the recommendations of the Guatemala Poverty Assessment Report, which suggest that preventive health measures be emphasized, targeted particularly to the following vulnerable groups: poor and malnourished children, poor women and girls, poor indigenous households, and the rural poor (World Bank 2003). In Guatemala, these groups are also most affected by IAP.

What Can Be Done about Indoor Air Pollution?

International academic journals contain a rich stock of papers on exposure monitoring experiments in Guatemala. The results of some of these are described in chapters 1 and 3. IAP was not a topic on the agenda of any government agency at the start of this project, however. As the study developed, a gradual understanding built, primarily through the dissemination workshops, of the importance of intersectoral collaboration on this issue and of the importance and emotive nature of the issue itself, which is so closely linked with the well-being of children and women, mainly in poor, rural, indigenous households, and with the country's poverty reduction goals. During the April 2003 workshop, participants identified a number of issues as barriers to successfully reducing IAP in rural homes:

- lack of a national policy
- lack of leadership
- apathy (as reflected by a lack of willingness on the part of the government to act and a lack of interest on the part of the population)

- lack of interinstitutional coordination
- resistance to change
- lack of education
- lack of training
- poverty and lack of access to resources
- lack of state policies

These barriers reflect the fact that there is a dire shortage of information about this topic and, as a result, an absence of a constituency prepared to act. The interventions described below aim to ensure availability of information so that the extent of the problem can be monitored, to facilitate solutions through better coordination and use of technical options, and to ensure sustainability in the implementation of options through the promotion of long-term behavioral change. At a broad level, four types of interventions are needed:

- *Monitoring the problem and improving understanding of the links between health and poverty reduction.* Building a constituency through the provision of information about the subject itself is an important intervention. Strong evidence indicates this problem is closely linked with Guatemala's poverty reduction agenda, but there are gaps in the evidence that need to be filled in. An improved stove intervention trial being conducted by Professor Kirk Smith and his co-workers, which aims to estimate the reduction in ALRI that can be achieved with improved stove use, will shed more light on the severity of the problem of IAP and ALRI in Guatemala and on the effectiveness of improved stoves as an intervention. The government needs to follow this study and other research in this area exploring the link between ALRI and pneumonia, and IAP. ALRI and pneumonia are the leading health issues with respect to both morbidity and mortality for children in Guatemala, and a better understanding of these links is important to guide national health policies.
- *Greater interinstitutional coordination.* Greater interinstitutional coordination is probably the most crucial intervention. The issue of IAP is spread across the mandates of different government institutions: for example, the technical mitigation options lie within the mandate of the Ministry of Energy and Mines, but the link with health impacts and dissemination of these impacts lies with the Ministry of Health. In terms of financial resources, the FIS has a major role in financing the technical options, such as improved stoves, for poor households. The technical innovation and health impact aspects are missing from its current program, however. This is a case where the sum of the parts clearly would have a greater impact than the cumulative impact of each part separately.

  Coordination of the various stakeholders is also crucial. These stakeholders consist of the government, with which the policy options and the broader mandate of poverty reduction lie; the private sector, which can help develop the market for the technical options, namely improved stoves and LPG in rural areas; nongovernmental organizations (NGOs), which can act as a partner to the government in the implementation of programs addressing health service delivery in rural areas and improved stoves; households, particularly the women who use the stove and the men who choose to buy it and often collect firewood for it; and academia, which is working on establishing a firm link between health and IAP.

A third layer of coordination is with Guatemala's neighbor to the north, Mexico, where 28 million people use firewood for cooking and where the same issues are under discussion. The main advantage of this collaboration would be the creation of a larger market for technical mitigation options and, therefore, one that would be more attractive to the private sector. Joint monitoring and sharing of research would also bring additional benefits for both countries.

- *Making people aware of the problem to promote behavioral change.* Lack of information and lack of an understanding of the link between smoke and poor health mean that there has been no constituency to champion change. The dissemination of the findings of this study has started to build a constituency at the level of the government stakeholders, but much more needs to be done. A striking finding of the stoves study was that women did not see the link between health and smoke. This clearly needs to change if behavioral change is to follow. Women's groups and NGOs can play an important role in getting the message to the final users. Revising government training and health outreach programs, as well as existing media campaigns for improved stoves and LPG, so that they also discuss the link between smoke and health could greatly help the promotion of long-term changes in behavior.
- *Implementing technical options.* Technical options—principally improved stoves for the lower income quintiles with targeted subsidies through the FIS, and uptake of improved stoves and LPG stoves for the higher income quintiles—need to be implemented. Most of the existing improved stoves programs (of which there are many, compared with other countries in Central America) focus on fuel efficiency, are highly subsidized, offer limited choice to the user, and are implemented in a modular manner, with no interaction between the government and its policies and the different suppliers. The design and implementation of the various programs also seem to follow separate rules. It is essential that the government take a more proactive role in establishing policies related to improved stoves programs. Such policies should emphasize both fuel efficiency and health impact as the key criteria for stove design, and should promote a market-based system that targets subsidies to the poorest and offers choice and training for the user. The implementation of such policies will require full coordination between the different government entities and other nongovernmental stakeholders.

Achievement of this level of coordination will require that an intersectoral coordination group on rural household energy be established, in which all key stakeholders are represented and that has as a mandate the championing and implementation of policies related to meeting the energy needs of rural families. It is particularly important that this mandate be closely linked with broader rural development programs, and that the group's efforts focus on improving the current infrastructure and programs rather than seeking to only create new programs. As a complement to the activities of an intersectoral coordination group, the Guatemalan Ministry of Energy and Mines should establish and lead a technical stoves unit. This unit should act on behalf of the consumer, to certify stoves on both efficiency and health grounds, and on behalf of the FIS, enabling it to offer users a choice of certified stoves (including perhaps an LPG option). Coordination on better house design to improve ventilation is another area for possible government intervention, through building codes and work with local municipal leaders. Donors and NGOs also need to ensure that their programs are in step with government efforts and that they are not operating modularly.

On the LPG front, the government needs to play a role in monitoring price movements to ensure that the current duopoly structure does not lead to high end-user prices, and should explore the option of introducing a system of cylinder ownership by firms, rather than by individuals, to accelerate cylinder renewal and to reduce accidents.

The budgetary implications of an intervention program cannot be ignored, particularly given the many pressing issues that the Guatemalan government faces. These suggested interventions seek to make current arrangements more efficient and effective in combating IAP, rather than introducing entirely new arrangements. In addition to a more targeted use of existing budgetary resources, additional financing will also be necessary. The new financing would have to cover the establishment of a technical stove unit and an increase in the number of staff in the Ministry of Health's Environment Unit involved with IAP monitoring and information dissemination. Given the close link between this issue and maternal and child health, it is expected that these increased costs would be offset in the longer term by improvements in health.

The sequencing of some of these events, if these recommendations are followed, is important. For example, the first move by the government would need to be the establishment of the intersectoral coordination group and technical stoves unit. Changes to the FIS program cannot precede this move.

These changes imply a change in the incentive framework under which all IAP stakeholders operate. Opening up the FIS program to more than one design would result in opening up the improved stoves market to several other market players, including regional players; this would increase the options for the user and, in the long term, would bring down the prices of improved stoves. It would also force the stove manufacturers to make more than one design, and would provide an incentive to NGOs to organize demand and to deliver the service. This would be a significant change from the current situation in which the manufacture of each different stove is the sole preserve of a single maker, and in which distinct stove programs are led by NGOs, typically supported by foreign donors. If the FIS were to offer a fixed subsidy amount for all certified improved stoves, the market could provide improved stoves (including LPG stoves) at different price levels, so that the user could make the choice between perhaps an expensive, large stove with a long life (such as the current FIS *plancha*) and a cheaper, small stove with a shorter life for which the FIS subsidy might cover the full cost.

The activities under this study were chosen to complement existing activities in Guatemala, and are therefore by no means comprehensive. The focus of the study has been to provide policy makers with information on the possible extent of the IAP problem in Guatemala. Particular emphasis has been given to policy recommendations to enhance the impact of existing improved stoves and LPG programs. Key areas requiring further investigation include the following:

- research into the changes in exposure to $PM_{2.5}$ (particulate matter with an aerodynamic diameter less than 2.5 microns) of different members of the household when using an improved stove under real conditions (with a focus on operation and maintenance of the stove), and the corresponding impact on health
- analysis of the costs and benefits of different mitigation options
- analysis of LPG availability and corresponding issues in rural areas
- assessment of current and planned rural development programs, and provision of recommendations based on worldwide experience on how best to integrate the technical options for mitigating IAP into the context of these programs

In conclusion, IAP must be made a priority in Guatemala. Despite the many knowledge gaps, there is a strong case that the government and other stakeholders should act to address this issue, in particular because of its close links to child mortality and maternal health.

Notes

1. Acute respiratory infection, ARI, may include acute lower respiratory tract infection (ALRI) or acute upper respiratory tract infection (AURI).

2. In clarification, ARI can be caused by a number of factors. Worldwide health studies suggest there is strong evidence of a link between IAP and ARI, particularly in small children.

3. Based on figures received from MSPAS. Note that these may be underrepresentative due to underreporting in some *departamentos*. Furthermore, trends are difficult to analyze because the increase may reflect improvements in the health surveillance system, rather than in epidemiological factors.

1
Introduction

Exposure to indoor air pollution (IAP) can be attributed to two principal sources. Historically, the most important sources have been cooking and household heating using solid fuels such as firewood, coal, manure, and agricultural waste. More recently, environmental tobacco smoke (ETS) has also been identified as a major source of exposure in industrial countries.

Recognition of the problems of IAP, and specifically of its harmful effects on health, is growing worldwide. Half the world's population is exposed to IAP, mainly through burning solid fuels for cooking and heating, and work is increasing to understand and articulate the complex links between health and air pollution and to address the health effects of IAP. Much evidence has been documented, for example, that associates biomass fuel combustion with the incidence of chronic bronchitis in women and of acute respiratory infection (ARI) in children (relevant references are cited in later sections of this report).

A World Health Organization (WHO) report concluded that consistent evidence exists that exposure to biomass smoke increases the risk of a range of common and serious diseases in both children and adults (WHO 2002). Most notable among these diseases are acute lower respiratory infections (ALRIs)[1] —in particular, pneumonia—in children. The report also identified IAP due to solid fuels as one of the 10 main risk factors behind a substantial proportion of the leading causes of death and disability. Indoor smoke from solid fuels causes an estimated 1.6 million deaths annually and accounts for 2.7 percent of the global burden of disease; global estimates also attribute 36 percent of all lower respiratory infections, 22 percent of chronic obstructive pulmonary disease (COPD), and 1.5 percent of trachea, bronchus, and lung cancer to IAP.

In rural areas especially, burning traditional fuels in ill-designed stoves or hearths exposes women and children to harmful concentrations of particulate matter and gaseous pollutants. Women who spend large amounts of time cooking and young children who spend time around these women are at risk in particular. The World Bank's Environmental Strategy for the Energy Sector estimated that, in developing countries, nearly 60 percent of premature deaths caused by local air pollution are children under the age of five who are exposed to pollution from dirty cooking fuels

1

(World Bank 1999). In high-mortality developing countries worldwide it is estimated that 3.7 percent of the disability-adjusted life years (DALYs)[2] lost to disease are due to indoor smoke from solid fuels. In high-mortality countries in the Americas, typically in Latin America, it is estimated that indoor smoke from solid fuels annually causes 10,000 deaths and 298,000 years of life lost (WHO 2002).

The literature and the experience of various countries indicate that mitigation of the health impacts of IAP can be achieved through moving up the energy ladder, from fuelwood to cleaner liquid or gaseous fuels, such as kerosene and liquefied petroleum gas (LPG), and ultimately to electricity. At the lower end of the energy ladder, better ventilation and the use of stoves that vent smoke through a chimney can decrease exposure to the harmful emission of pollutants. Figure 1.1 illustrates these different fuel and technology options. The policies that would facilitate the spread of these options are cross-sectoral, and include fuel pricing and distribution policies, small business development, income generation activities, and health education. Behavioral and cultural factors are also important when considering technical mitigation options to achieve positive health effects. Together with the barrier posed by a lack of information, these factors are often the greatest barriers that need to be addressed.

Figure 1.1 Energy Options, Ranked by Increasing Effectiveness in Mitigating the Health Impacts of IAP

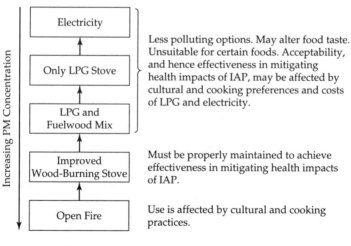

Source: Author.
PM = particulate matter
LPG = liquefied petroleum gas

Nature of the Problem in Guatemala

To provide a background to understanding the nature of the problem of health impacts of IAP in Guatemala, the following sections review the literature on exposure monitoring and statistics on morbidity and mortality due to ARI in Guatemala. Furthermore, the importance of the problem in Guatemala is underscored based on the specific context of the country including the close link between IAP and poverty, levels of rural electrification, and traditional fuel use.

ALRI and Exposure Monitoring in Guatemala

Recent statistics (table 1.1) from the Ministry of Public Health and Social Assistance (Ministerio de Salud Publica y Asistencia Social; MSPAS) in Guatemala indicate that between 1997 and 2000 ARI was the country's single most important cause of morbidity and mortality. In this period the number of cases of morbidity due to ARI grew by an average of 31 percent per year. ARI caused on average two to three times as many deaths as acute diarrhea, the second most important cause of mortality in Guatemala.

As a subset of these data, the impact of ARI on the health of children is particularly important. In 1997–2000, pneumonia was the single most important cause of infant death in Guatemala, accounting for 36 percent of all registered deaths among infants in 2000.

Table 1.1 Five Principal Causes of General Morbidity and Five Principal Causes of Mortality in Guatemala, 1997–2000

Morbidity *(per 1,000 habitants)*	*1997*	*1998*	*1999*	*2000*
ARI	**54.0**	**70.2**	103.3	**118.7**
Intestinal parasites	23.6	34.5	39.2	44.5
Acute diarrhea	17.0	28.2	31.1	45.1
Pneumonia and bronchial pneumonia	14.8	20.4	23.0	21.6
Anemia	8.8	11.7	19.6	29.1
Mortality *(per 10,000 habitants)*				
Pneumonias	**10.5**	**11.2**	10.8	**9.6**
Acute diarrhea	4.2	5.6	2.9	3.6
Malnutrition	1.6	1.5	1.6	1.5
Cancer	1.5	1.5	1.5	1.5
Acute heart attack	1.8	1.2	1.5	2.0

Source: MSPAS, Guatemala.

With the exception of a few individual efforts, activities in the Latin America and Caribbean region directed to the study of IAP have been relatively limited. In Guatemala, work on the health impacts of IAP notably includes measurement of the IAP concentrations associated with various types of fuel (see Smith and others 1993, Smith and others 2000, and McCracken and Smith 1998, among others).

In 1992, WHO established a committee to examine the feasibility of conducting controlled intervention studies to assess the effects on key child and adult respiratory health outcomes of a measured reduction in exposure to particulate pollution from biomass fuel cooking. WHO subsequently sponsored several pilot studies in the western highlands of Guatemala, with the objective of determining the risk-reduction potential of various interventions such as fuel substitution, stove alteration, improved ventilation, and behavior modification (Bruce and others 1998; McCracken and Smith 1998; Neufeld 1995; Smith and others 1993). Some of these studies and their findings are described below.

Bruce and others (1998) examined the association between respiratory symptoms and the use of open fires compared with the use of improved wood-burning stoves with chimneys (or *planchas*). The study sample was a cross-section of 340 women ages 15–45 living in a poor, rural area in the western highlands of Guatemala. This study used direct measures of exposure, and sought to address the issue of confounding by systematically examining the extent to which strong associations with confounding variables in the study settings limited the ability of observational studies to adequately define the effects of IAP. The study found that the prevalence of reported cough and phlegm was significantly higher for three of six symptom measures among women using open fires compared to those using *planchas*. Strong associations were also found between the type of fire and a number of household and socioeconomic factors, including the arrangement of rooms, floor type, and possession of a radio or television. This study concluded that although a reasonable case for causal association existed, confounding presented a substantial problem for observational studies of IAP and health. It concluded, therefore, that intervention studies were required to convincingly demonstrate such association and, more importantly, to determine the magnitude of the health benefit achievable through feasible exposure reductions.

McCracken and Smith (1998) compared the thermal efficiency and emissions of the traditional three-stone fire and the *plancha*. This study reported no statistical difference between the efficiency of the *plancha* and the traditional stove, but reported a significant difference in the emission of suspended particles and carbon monoxide (CO), the *plancha* emitting far fewer of the pollutants than the open fire.

Naeher and others (2000) conducted a study in the western Guatemalan highlands to determine if the IAP levels in several villages made them viable candidates for an intervention study monitoring $PM_{2.5}$ (particulate matter with an aerodynamic diameter of less than 2.5 microns) and CO during breakfast, lunch, and dinner in three high-density and four low-density villages. The study also investigated the impact of neighborhood pollution on IAP levels, and characterized indoor concentrations for different meals and stoves. The predominant stove type was the open fire, but several other stoves, in various levels of disrepair, were observed. The findings demonstrated a significant difference in indoor concentrations during cooking times for the different stoves used. The highest concentrations of $PM_{2.5}$, averaging 5.31 mg/m^3, were observed in homes using an open fire or equivalent, but measurements in excess of 13.8 mg/m^3 were also observed in homes using the *plancha*. The highest indoor concentrations of CO, averaging 22.9 ppm (parts per million) were similarly observed in homes using open fires. The maximum measurement observed was in excess of 250 ppm. Levels of $PM_{2.5}$ and CO measured in homes with the *plancha*, Lorena stove (an indigenous stove made in Guatemala that pre-dates the *plancha* and is made of earth and sand), or open fire were significantly higher than the levels recorded in the street or in homes using a gas stove. From an exposure-based assessment perspective, the study concluded that the region was a viable area in which to conduct an epidemiological intervention study of the association between biomass fuel combustion and ARI and other health effects in women and children. The variation of indoor levels of $PM_{2.5}$ and CO in homes using *planchas* additionally suggested the need for closer monitoring of exposures in households with *planchas*.

In another study, Naeher, Leaderer, and Smith (2000) examined the effectiveness of various stoves in reducing IAP. The study assessed indoor and outdoor pollution levels, primarily of particulate matter and CO, associated with traditional and improved wood stoves and gas stoves, taking measurements in kitchens, bedrooms, and outdoors in three test homes before and after the introduction of potential exposure-reducing interventions. With nine observations, these studies found that kitchen $PM_{2.5}$, PM_{10} (particulate matter with an aerodynamic diameter less than 10 microns), and CO levels for open fire conditions were consistently higher than for *plancha* and gas stove conditions. Kitchen $PM_{2.5}$ levels were 56 μg/m^3 under background conditions, 528 μg/m^3 for open fire conditions, 96 μg/m^3 for *plancha* conditions, and 57μg/m^3 for gas stove conditions. Corresponding PM_{10}/TSP (total suspended particles) levels were 173/174, 717/836, 210/276, 186/218 μg/m^3, and corresponding CO levels were 0.2, 5.9, 1.4, and 1.2 ppm (see table 1.2). Comparisons with other studies in the area indicated that reductions in indoor concentrations achieved by improved wood-burning stoves deteriorate with stove age. The study concluded that the use of better wood stoves with flues and of gas stoves reduced exposure to 10 to 20 percent of that observed in kitchens using open fires for cooking.

Particulate matter would be the best indicator of pollutant risks from fuel combustion for studies of childhood ARI, but the large scale, long duration,

Table 1.2 Comparison of Indoor Pollution Levels from Open Fire, *Plancha*, and LPG Stove in the Guatemalan Highlands

	Indoor concentration of pollutant		
Type of stove	$PM_{2.5}$ ($\mu g/m^3$)	PM_{10} ($\mu g/m^3$)	CO (mg/m^3)
Open fire	527 (248.5)	717 (284.6)	5.9
Plancha	96.5 (66.5)	186.3 (89.5)	1.4
LPG stove	56.8 (19.0)	210.2 (100.3)	1.2

Source: Naeher, Leaderer, and Smith 2000.

Note: $PM_{2.5}$ and PM_{10} = Particulate matter with an aerodynamic diameter less than 2.5 microns and 10 microns, respectively. Numbers in parentheses are standard deviations.

and difficult logistics of such studies make the widespread use of particulate monitoring complicated and expensive. Naeher and others (2001) investigated efficient and effective $PM_{2.5}$ measurements and examined how personal measurements relate to area measurements. The study showed that CO is a strong proxy for $PM_{2.5}$ exposure in homes using open fires or *planchas*, but that its use as a proxy is not valid under gas stove use or similarly clean-burning conditions. This finding was in agreement with McCracken and Smith (1998). The study also reported that a mother's personal CO exposure is strongly correlated with that of her child (less than age two), suggesting that mother personal CO exposure monitoring can be used as a proxy for child CO exposure monitoring. The study demonstrated that area CO measurements are not representative of personal CO measurements.

Albalak and others (2001) measured the indoor respirable particulate matter concentrations caused by open fire, *plancha*, and LPG and open fire combination in a rural Guatemalan community. The study included 30 households and compared $PM_{3.5}$ concentrations over eight months in each situation. Its findings showed a 45 percent lower $PM_{3.5}$ concentration for the LPG and open fire combination than for the open fire alone. The *plancha* showed an 85 percent lower $PM_{3.5}$ concentration compared to the open fire. The $PM_{3.5}$ concentrations were not affected by time or season.

Emerging from the background of pilot and other studies that have been conducted in Guatemala is a recently initiated intervention study, financed by the U.S. National Institutes of Health, being conducted by Kirk Smith and colleagues in the San Marcos area of the Guatemalan highlands. Some of the studies described above were included in the feasibility studies that were used to design Smith's intervention study. The study is expected to last two years, and hopes to achieve the following:

- reduction or elimination of the confusing variables in the IAP-health nexus that are due to random design selection

- quantification of risks to permit the direct measurement of exposure
- standard definition of cases and thorough confirmation of cases in the community
- direct proof of the effects on health of an accepted and practical intervention in the area

The Country Context

The preceding section indicates that ARI and pneumonia are the leading causes of morbidity and mortality in Guatemala, and describes the work under way to show the extent of the links between these diseases and IAP. Equally important, however, is the country context and the close linkage between IAP and poverty, levels of rural electrification, and traditional fuel use. In Guatemala, IAP arises from the burning of fuelwood, typically on a three-stone fire. The rural poor are disproportionately affected by IAP because they have no alternative to the use of fuelwood, because they are not connected with the electricity grid, or cannot afford cleaner fuels. The recent Guatemala Poverty Assessment Report provides the following country-level data on these factors (World Bank 2003):

- *High incidence of poverty.* In 2000, more than half of all Guatemalans (56 percent, or about 6.4 million people) lived in poverty, and at a level that suggests that poverty is higher than in other Central American countries, despite Guatemala's mid-range ranking using per capita GDP.
- *Low levels of rural electrification.* Access to modern utility services is highly inequitable. While access to electricity is almost universal in urban areas, the grid reaches little more than half of rural households. Fewer than 40 percent of the poorest households have electricity connection, compared to 95 percent of the richest households.
- *Large rural populations.* More than 60 percent of the Guatemalan population lives in rural areas. Poverty in Guatemala is predominantly rural and extreme poverty[3] is almost exclusively rural. Eighty-one percent of the poor and 93 percent of the extreme poor live in the countryside. Three-quarters of all rural residents fall below the full poverty line,[4] and one-quarter live in extreme poverty.
- *High levels of traditional fuel use.* Fuelwood is the dominant cooking fuel in 97 percent of households in rural areas. Among rural households, 42 percent use fuelwood only, and 55 percent practice multiple fuel use.

The Poverty Assessment Report identifies five priority groups to which poverty reduction efforts should be targeted:

- poor and malnourished children, especially in the age groups 0–6 years and 7–13 years

- poor girls and women
- poor indigenous households
- the rural poor
- specific geographic areas, notably in the "poverty belt" (the northern and northwestern regions and the *departamento* of San Marcos)

In the rural Guatemalan highlands, approximately 400,000 children under age five live in homes in which open fires are used for cooking. The risks of ARI are increased by poverty, inadequate dwellings, overcrowding, malnutrition, deficiency of micronutrients, indoor and outdoor air pollution, and environmental tobacco smoke. These findings underscore the strategic importance and timeliness of a study to improve the understanding of the impact of IAP on the health of vulnerable groups in Guatemala and to assess the policy options for mitigating these impacts.

Context for This Report

The study reported here was carried out between October 2001 and June 2003 with support from ESMAP (Energy Sector Management Assistance Program). This report summarizes the findings of each of a series of substudies, as well as of two workshops, and presents final recommendations.

The two objectives of this study were to estimate the health impacts of traditional fuel use and to outline strategies and policies for mitigating the environmental health damage due to household fuel use. Mitigation of IAP from the use of traditional biomass fuels is identified in the World Bank's *Fuel for Thought: Environmental Strategy for the Energy Sector* as a high priority (World Bank 1999). In addition, given the close linkages between IAP and women's and children's health, this study provides information for the government of Guatemala that relates to its pursuit of the Millennium Development Goals of reducing child mortality and improving maternal health.

The study, conducted in response to a request by the Guatemalan Ministry of Energy and Mines, is the first of its type conducted by the World Bank in Latin America and the Caribbean. The rich source of data on the subject of IAP and health; the close link between IAP and poverty; and the potential replicability for applying the lessons learned through this work to other Central American countries that face similar issues, were important considerations in carrying out this study.

Individual Studies

The major activities included individual studies of specific aspects of the IAP and health matrix, and two dissemination workshops. Four specific studies were carried out under the overall study:

- a review of the literature on IAP and health globally and in Guatemala, and an estimate of the health implications of not addressing the problem of ARIs and IAP, either through policy interventions or technical mitigation measures
- a review of two major surveys conducted in Guatemala—the 1998–99 Demographic and Health Survey (DHS), and the 2000 Living Standards Measurement Study (LSMS)—to investigate the potential relationship between energy use and IAP
- an evaluation of improved stoves programs in Guatemala, and a focused review of the cost structure of providing stoves under such programs
- a study of the LPG industry and market in Guatemala

These activities were chosen to complement activities that were under way in Guatemala at the time, including a Poverty Assessment financed by the Bank, an ESMAP-sponsored network in Central America on Women and Improved Stoves, and exposure monitoring through an intervention study financed by the U.S. National Institutes of Health. In addition, at the time of the study the Bank and other development partners were providing support to the Social Investment Fund (Fondo de Inversión Social; FIS), which included, as one component in a menu of poverty reduction actions, the largest improved stoves program in Guatemala. (This study includes a review of and corresponding policy recommendations to enhance the impact of this particular program, with respect to reducing IAP).

This study is by no means comprehensive. Potential future areas of investigation include the following:

- analysis of the changes in exposure to $PM_{2.5}$ of different members of a household upon introduction of an improved stove under real conditions (with a focus on both operation and maintenance of the stove), and the corresponding impact on health
- analysis of the costs and benefits of different mitigation options
- analysis of LPG availability and corresponding issues in rural areas
- assessment of rural development programs to establish, based on worldwide experience, how best to integrate the technical options for mitigating IAP in the context of these programs

Structure of the Report

Chapters 2 through 5 describe the findings and recommendations of the four studies listed in this chapter. Chapter 2 presents the results of an exploratory study, based on two large household surveys conducted between 1998 and 2000, and attempts to examine the links between energy use and health. Chapter 3 presents a review of exposure-monitoring studies in

Guatemala and attempts to carry out some informal estimates (based on worldwide IAP health studies) of the health implications of not addressing the problem of ARIs and IAP, either through policy interventions or technical mitigation measures. Chapter 4 examines one of the most active stove programs in Central America. Chapter 5 assesses the LPG market in Guatemala, to gain a better understanding of some of the current and potential future problems that might discourage households from using LPG. Finally, chapter 6 summarizes our policy recommendations, incorporating feedback from the two workshops, and emphasizes the need for a multisectoral approach to address this issue, which is so closely linked with the Millennium Development Goals and Guatemala's development.

Notes

1. Acute respiratory infection (ARI) may comprise acute lower respiratory infection (ALRI) or acute upper respiratory infection (AURI).

2. The DALY is a standard metric of the burden of disease. DALYs combine life years lost as a result of illness and disability, with one DALY being equal to the loss of one healthy life year (Murray and López 1996).

3. The extreme poverty line is defined by the yearly cost of a food basket that provides the minimum daily requirement of 2,172 calories (World Bank 2003).

4. The full poverty line is defined as the extreme poverty line plus an allowance for nonfood items (World Bank 2003).

2

Indoor Air Pollution and Health: Evidence from the Demographic and Health Survey and the Living Standards Measurement Study

Inhaling smoke from wood combustion affects human health in ways that depend on the levels and degree of exposure. Smoke inhalation is, for example, one of the main causes of death due to respiratory complications following fires (Dantzker and Scharf 2000). The effects of inhalation can be temporary or chronic, can generate permanent lesions as bronchitis does, or can cause infections such as pneumonia. In the absence of proper care, complications of any of these pathologies can cause death. In Latin America there has been little study of the health effects of indoor air pollution (IAP), although voices of alert on the subject can be traced back at least two decades in local medical literature (Restrepo and others 1983). Studies in Nicaragua have recently shown that acute respiratory infections (ARIs), in many cases linked to fuelwood smoke exposure, are the second leading cause of death among infants, after diarrhea. Respiratory illnesses associated with IAP are also one of the main burdens of disease treated by the public health system: The cost of treating ARIs directly caused by fuelwood smoke reaches a conservative minimum estimate of US$4 million annually in Nicaragua.

The purpose of this chapter is to present the results of a study that examines the relationship between the use of different types of fuels and the implications for the health of women and children in Guatemala. This is an exploratory study based on two large household surveys conducted during the years 2000 and 1998–99. Both of these household surveys provide indicators and measures of both health and energy use. The goal is to examine any links between energy use and health for Guatemala. This is complementary to ongoing major work being completed in Guatemala on this topic (see Boy, Bruce, and Delgado 2002; Bruce, Neufeld, Boy, and West 1998; Boy, Bruce, Smith, and Hernández 2000).

The Survey Samples

The two main data sources used for this study were the 2000 Living Standards Measurement Study (LSMS) published by World Bank/INE/UN (2000) and the 1998–1999 Demographic and Health Survey (DHS) for Guatemala (Macro International 1999). The LSMS is a multipurpose survey that is used as the basis of the World Bank country poverty assessments. The DHS survey, which collects information mainly on children under age five and the women who take care of them, has become a fairly standardized approach to evaluating issues of health, mortality, and fertility in developing countries. The data from these surveys are analyzed to assess the impact of the use of various types of energy or the use of particular stoves on health in Guatemala. Both of these surveys are weak when used for such analysis, but the results are suggestive with regard both to substantive findings and to implications for areas of further research.

The DHS Sample

For the 1998–1999 DHS survey, 5,587 households representing 30,874 family members were interviewed on issues involving the health of women and children in the family. A total of 6,756 women between the ages of 15 and 49 were interviewed. The survey also provided information on 4,943 children born during the previous five years, of which about 5 percent had died. The survey sample was designed to be representative at the national and regional levels. Although the number of interviews in several of the regions was small compared to population size (particularly metropolitan Guatemala, which provided 8.1 percent of the sample compared to 32.9 percent of the universe), the results are representative of the country as a whole. (See table 2.1.)

The survey coverage for metropolitan areas in Guatemala is somewhat low, but this was probably due to a greater policy interest in rural health and demographic issues. For descriptive analysis, care must to be taken to weight each case by its corresponding weighting factor. The major weakness of the DHS data for this study is the lack of information on household income or expenditures. A wealth index composed of various types of household assets is used as a proxy for income, but while this is useful for many types of studies it raises a problem for the analysis carried out in this chapter, because it encompasses within the index the type of stove and energy used by each household.

The LSMS Sample

The sample for the LSMS study was designed to be representative nationally and regionally. The LSMS is a multipurpose survey of which health is just a small component. A total of 7,276 households, representing 37,926

Table 2.1 Sample Distribution: Guatemala 1998–1999 DHS

| | Region | | | | | | | | |
Results	Metropolitan	North	Northeast	Southeast	Central	Southwest	Northwest	Petén	Total
Actual sample									
Households interviewed	455	413	640	399	752	1,152	703	1,073	5,587
Individuals	2,302	2,319	3,294	2,161	3,827	6,597	4,182	6,192	30,874
Eligible women (ages 15–49)	599	507	737	456	862	1,463	906	1,226	6,756
Weighted sample									
Households interviewed	1,840	362	502	499	580	1,103	549	152	5,587
Eligible women (ages 15–49)	2,112	389	481	490	571	1,208	617	152	6,021
Household distribution (%)									
Unweighted results	8.1	7.4	11.5	7.1	13.5	20.6	12.6	19.2	100.0
Weighted results	32.9	6.5	9.0	8.9	10.4	19.7	9.8	2.7	100.0

Source: DHS (Macro International 1999).

Note: The unweighted results summarize the information from the survey based on sample households, and the weighted results provide weights to the sample households so that the averages are representative of figures for Guatemala.

individuals, were surveyed for the *Encuesta Nacional sobre Condiciones de Vida 2000* (World Bank, INE, and United Nations 2000), distributed by region and urban and rural breakdown as shown in table 2.2. The survey covered 6,074 children under age five.

In contrast to the DHS survey, one of the main features of the LSMS is that it explicitly measures household income, consumer expenditure, and poverty levels. It also includes detailed questions on energy use, the type of kitchen and stoves used by the household, and additional variables related to IAP that are not investigated by the DHS. For example, the survey measures each fuel used for cooking, along with the time spent cooking on the previous day by each household member. This can serve as a proxy for exposure to IAP, particularly for young infants who typically spend much of their time with their mothers. The treatment of health in the LSMS, and especially of ARI, is much less specific than in the DHS.

Each survey thus has both strong and weak points in relation to its applicability to this analysis. The LSMS is strong on the measurement of social and economic characteristics of rural households, but is relatively weak in terms of its attention to health issues. The DHS is strong on the measurement of women's and children's health, but is fairly weak in its examination of the socioeconomic characteristics of the families surveyed.

Socioeconomic Profile

While the two surveys differ in their sampling and questioning techniques, they have enough variables in common to enable joint presentation of the socioeconomic and energy use aspects that they assess. This section highlights those socioeconomic aspects considered most relevant to the analysis of IAP and infant health.

The urban-rural distribution of households by region indicates that roughly 56 percent of the population in Guatemala is rural and 44 percent urban. The average urban household in Guatemala has between 4.67 (DHS) and 4.97 (LSMS) members. Rural households averaged 5.7 members in both surveys. Between 18.4 percent and 19.5 percent of households overall are headed by women, with the proportion of female-headed households slightly higher in urban settings (23.1 percent according to LSMS and 23.7 percent according to DHS).

The level of household income and poverty was examined only in the LSMS. According to the LSMS, only 1.7 percent of the urban population can be classified as extremely poor, compared to 17.8 percent of the rural population. The national average is 10.8 percent. Non-extreme poverty in urban areas affects 18.3 percent of the population, compared to 47.8 percent in rural areas. While only 34.4 percent of Guatemala's rural population is classified as nonpoor, this level of well-being has been reached by 80 percent of the country's urban population. The incidence of extreme

Table 2.2 Sample Distribution: Guatemala 2000 LSMS

LSMS Sample	Region								
	Metropolitan	North	Northeast	Southeast	Central	Southwest	Northwest	Petén	Total
Unweighted results (thousands)									
Urban households	807	392	375	326	427	427	404	266	3,424
Urban persons	3,431	1,916	1,658	1,575	2,048	2,128	2,120	1,312	16,188
Rural households	119	406	224	479	824	688	793	319	3,852
Rural persons	596	2,419	1,114	2,581	4,304	3,925	4,881	1,918	21,738
Total households	926	798	599	805	1,251	1,115	1,197	585	7,276
Total persons	4,027	4,335	2,772	4,156	6,352	6,053	7,001	3,230	37,926
Weighted results (thousands)									
Urban households	480	29	53	46	112	161	46	20	951
Urban persons	2,113	146	241	230	540	818	246	102	4,441
Rural households	70	129	139	141	129	386	198	44	1,239
Rural persons	387	773	693	769	682	2,212	1,223	269	7,012
Total households	551	159	192	188	242	547	244	65	2,191
Total persons	2,501	919	935	999	1,222	3,030	1,470	372	11,453
Percent distribution									
Urban									
Sample	23.6	11.4	11.0	9.5	12.5	12.5	11.8	7.8	100
Universe	50.5	3.1	5.6	4.9	11.9	16.9	4.9	2.2	100
Rural									
Sample	3.1	10.5	5.8	12.4	21.4	17.9	20.6	8.3	100
Universe	5.7	10.5	11.3	11.4	10.4	31.2	16.0	3.6	100
Total									
Sample	12.7	11.0	8.2	11.1	17.2	15.3	16.5	8.0	100
Universe	25.2	7.3	8.8	8.6	11.1	25.0	11.2	3.0	100

Source: LSMS data files (World Bank/INE/UN 2000).

Note: The unweighted results summarize the information from the survey based on sample households, and the weighted results provide weights to the sample households so that the averages are representative of figures for Guatemala.

poverty is highest in the rural areas of the north (35.7 percent) and northwest (28.2 percent), but in absolute terms 29.1 percent of the country's rural extreme poor live in the southwest, followed by the northwest (25.3 percent) and north (21.0 percent).

In the absence of income data in the DHS, analysts such as Filmer and Pritchett (1998) established that from the standard list of household assets and basic services (such as running water and garbage disposal) obtained by such surveys, it is possible to generate an "asset index" as a proxy for relative household wealth. Thus, a household asset index was developed from the LSMS data that is similar to the index used by the DHS. The percentage of the total variance explained by the DHS-style wealth index is about 28 percent for income per person, 22 percent for family income in the country, and less for rural households.[1] The DHS index as a proxy for family income therefore does have some weaknesses.

The relationship between parental education and childcare, child health, and infant survival rates is important. Both studies in general indicate less formal schooling among mothers than fathers and less educational attainment among parents in rural households than in urban homes. Both also show the highest schooling among parents to exist in metropolitan Guatemala and the lowest schooling to exist in the northwest and north.

Around 76 percent of Guatemalan households live in homes of their own. Home ownership is particularly high in rural areas, and less so in urban areas, especially the metropolitan region, where rented homes are more common. The construction materials used are good indicators of relative well-being or quality of life. For example, more than 50 percent of rural households and approximately 20 percent of urban households live in homes with earth floors. Regionally, earth floors are predominant in the north (72 percent) northwest (68–69 percent), and Petén. These three regions generally lag behind the others for all socioeconomic indicators, with the metropolitan area generally showing the strongest indicators.

The amenities in the home can also have a significant impact on family health. Electricity is available to slightly more than 70 percent of Guatemalan households; but where urban coverage surpasses 90 percent, the electrification of rural households reaches only about 55 percent. The region with the highest coverage is the metropolitan area, with the north, Petén, and the northwest again lagging for this indicator (table 2.3). Approximately 42 percent of all households still use traditional pit latrines and 13 percent have no toilet facilities at all. Approximately 80 percent of all households possess radios. Access to television is widespread: around 80 percent among urban households and 37 percent among rural homes, for a national average of about 55 percent. Telephone coverage is sparse (less than 7 percent in rural areas and only 17 percent nationally). Few households own cars or motorcycles.

Table 2.3 Guatemalan Households with Electricity
percent

	Survey	
Area	*1998–1999 DHS*	*2000 LSMS*
Total	70.9	73.1
Urban	91.4	95.4
Rural	54.0	56.4
Region		
Metropolitan	91.0	95.8
North	33.1	30.1
Northeast	59.3	62.9
Southeast	73.0	69.9
Central	73.3	80.4
Southwest	72.0	76.1
Northwest	43.6	56.5
Petén	30.9	36.0

Source: LSMS (World Bank/INE/UN 2000). DHS (Macro International 1999).

Household Energy Use and IAP Factors

Cooking with fuelwood under poor ventilation conditions has been demonstrated in the literature to be associated with a higher risk of infant mortality or morbidity due to ARI. Most of the evidence for this is based on detailed case studies with small sample sizes. In national surveys, the number of cases of ARI is much larger and more representative of whole populations, but the precision of definition of physical, technical, or family parameters is weak because the questionnaires do not specifically address these issues. The DHS and LSMS pursue many other objectives and were not designed specifically to measure the effect of IAP on health, and as such do not directly measure pollution. They do, however, measure factors that are associated with IAP, such as the types of fuels used for cooking, the types of kitchens, the existence of chimneys to vent smoke, and (for the LSMS) the amount of time spent cooking per day by household members older than age seven.

The DHS study contains questions on the "main fuel" used for cooking, and has established these as fuelwood and LPG. The use of electricity, kerosene, and other fuels as the primary cooking fuel extends to only about 1 percent of households countrywide (table 2.4). In urban areas LPG has supplanted fuelwood as a cooking fuel (in metropolitan Guatemala more than 75 percent of households use LPG), but in far rural areas fuelwood continues to dominate, being used in about 97 percent of homes in the north, 96 percent in the northwest, 93 percent in Petén, and 90 percent in the southwest. However, because the preponderance of the rural population

Table 2.4 Distribution of Main or Single Fuels Used for Cooking in Guatemala from 1998–1999 DHS

percent

Main Fuel	Region								
	Metropolitan	North	Northeast	Southeast	Central	Southwest	Northwest	Petén	Total
Urban									
Wood	22.3	41.5	37.5	50.4	36.8	39.3	76.1	59.7	31.6
Clean fuels	77.7	58.5	62.5	49.5	63.1	60.7	23.9	40.3	68.4
Kerosene	0.9	1.9	1.6	1.2	1.1	0.5	1.0	1.0	1.0
LPG	75.4	55.1	54.6	43.9	60.0	59.1	21.9	38.8	65.4
Electricity	1.4	1.5	0.3	1.5	0.2	0.2	1.0	—	1.1
Other	—	—	6.0	2.9	1.8	0.9	—	0.5	0.9
Rural									
Wood	17.9	97.3	85.7	73.8	74.4	90.1	96.4	92.7	77.8
Clean fuels	82.0	2.6	14.4	26.1	25.6	10.0	3.5	7.3	22.2
Kerosene	—	—	0.4	0.7	—	0.3	—	0.4	0.2
LPG	78.3	2.3	13.2	24.0	23.9	9.1	3.2	6.4	20.8
Electricity	2.8	—	0.8	—	—	0.2	—	—	0.5
Other	0.9	0.3	—	1.4	1.7	0.4	0.3	0.5	0.7
Total									
Wood	21.3	85.7	68.1	66.2	57.3	75.2	93.5	85.7	57.0
Clean fuels	78.8	14.3	31.9	33.9	42.7	24.8	6.4	14.3	43.0
Kerosene	0.7	0.4	0.8	0.9	0.5	0.3	0.1	0.5	0.5
LPG	76.1	13.3	28.3	30.6	40.3	23.7	5.9	13.3	40.9
Electricity	1.8	0.3	0.6	0.5	0.1	0.2	0.1	—	0.8
Other	0.2	0.3	2.2	1.9	1.8	0.6	0.3	0.5	0.8

Source: Weighted sample estimate from DHS data source provided by Macro International 1999.

Note: The weighted sample means that the figures are representative for the regions.

lives in near-urban areas, where LPG use is strong, the national average of rural homes that use clean fuels is 22 percent.

The LSMS for Guatemala took a different approach to determining the fuels that are used for cooking. Instead of asking about the "main cooking fuel," the LSMS posed questions on whether the household had used a fuel for cooking during the last month, regardless of the level of its use (table 2.5). This allowed households using more than one fuel to give more than one answer. In this survey, it was found that approximately 95 percent of rural households and, remarkably, 45 percent of urban households use some fuelwood for cooking. LPG is used by 78 percent of urban households, including 83 percent in the metropolitan areas. In rural areas, more than 20 percent of households use LPG to some extent, but as indicated for the DHS study the pattern of use is influenced by rural people residing in or near the metropolitan area. Kerosene is used for cooking by more than 8 percent of rural households and by almost 25 percent of urban households. The implications of this simultaneous use of various fuels are somewhat complex, but represent how people really cook in Guatemala.

To discern the role of each fuel in satisfying cooking needs and to begin to clarify the health implications, this study estimates the distribution of different fuel combinations used by urban and rural households in each of the country's regions. In urban areas, between 37 percent and 49 percent of households simultaneously use fuelwood and LPG or other clean cooking fuels, in proportions that cannot be discerned from these data. It is also impossible to accurately assess if the two fuels are used daily and for how much time, but recent studies in urban Nicaragua provide some insight into this by taking into account financial considerations and the types of foods consumed. For example, beans are a staple of the typical Guatemalan diet, and cooking beans requires four or more hours once or twice a week. For many households it would therefore be cheaper to cook beans with fuelwood, with LPG used for other foods such as rice or meats.

Most rural households rely solely on fuelwood for their cooking needs (69 percent), and few have made the switch to solely clean fuels (3 percent). Nonetheless, it is becoming more usual for rural households, as for their urban counterparts, to combine the use of fuelwood with clean fuels. This combining of fuels now ranges from 7 percent in Petén and 8 percent in the north to almost 38 percent in the northeast and metropolitan regions. In many rural areas of Latin America, where firewood generally is self-collected and thus is perceived as "free," dual-fuel households are common, with the clean fuel used for quick cooking, such as the preparation of breakfasts for children going off to school or for heating water, and fuelwood used for all other cooking. In conclusion, the LSMS results on cooking fuels seem to indicate that the DHS, by ignoring the fact that approximately two out of every three consumers maintains at least some reliance on fuelwood, overestimates the use of clean fuels in Guatemala.

Table 2.5 Summary of All Fuels Used for Cooking by Guatemalan Households

percent

Fuels used	Urban	Rural	Metropolitan	North	Northeast	Southeast	Central	Southwest	Northwest	Petén	Total
						Region					
Fuelwood	45.2	95.4	32.0	94.0	77.9	89.7	79.8	87.9	95.3	92.1	73.6
Kerosene	1.4	8.4	0.8	7.3	8.9	6.2	5.6	7.4	2.9	18.3	5.4
LPG	78.0	20.3	82.9	15.4	45.9	31.9	49.2	35.8	13.9	22.3	45.3
Charcoal	24.6	3.4	31.0	1.6	11.1	5.8	12.4	5.7	3.3	2.4	12.6
Electricity	4.8	0.8	4.1	1.0	4.9	1.8	2.6	1.7	1.9	0.7	2.5
Other	3.1	11.5	2.7	2.5	8.2	5.3	2.1	15.1	16.1	1.4	7.9

Source: LSMS (World Bank/INE/UN 2000).

Other factors influencing exposure to IAP include the type of kitchen used and ventilation. While neither the DHS nor the LSMS provides information on room sizes or the presence of windows, both classify the type of kitchen and ask whether chimneys are used. The data show that close to 80 percent of households, both urban and rural, have a kitchen used exclusively for cooking. The other 20 percent of households live either in single-room dwellings or cook in rooms that are also used for other purposes, thus increasing the exposure to fuelwood smoke. Despite progress in the implementation of the improved stoves program, it is uncommon for kitchens to have chimneys.

For assessing IAP levels, households (with any kind of kitchen) that use a clean fuel are combined into a single category with households that have an outdoor kitchen and that use any kind of fuel (table 2.6). Among urban households, about 40 percent can be classified as having low exposure levels; among rural households the figure is about 6 percent. Conditions of highest exposure—that is, cooking with fuelwood within a space shared with other household activities—are present in 20 percent of rural households.

The exposure of women and children to cooking smoke is an important health issue for Guatemala. The time spent by male family members cooking is negligible. Females, noticeably the mothers in the household, perform most of the cooking, and most mothers who depend solely on fuelwood spend more time cooking than those who use a mixture of clean and dirty fuels (and all spend more time than those who use only clean fuels). The women who use only fuelwood spend between 2.01 and 3.04 hours per day cooking, compared to 1.45 to 2.34 hours spent by those who use modern fuels. Given the childcare patterns observed by Naeher and others (2000) in Guatemalan villages, it is possible that infants younger than 12 or 15 months could be exposed to high concentrations of carbon monoxide (CO) and particulates for much of the 2.26 hours on average that their mothers spend cooking.

Infant Respiratory Illness Analysis and the National Surveys

The ultimate objective of this study is to explore the data generated by Guatemala's national DHS and LSMS surveys for evidence of the differential effects that exposure to IAP, or more specifically, to fuelwood smoke, might have on infant mortality and respiratory illness. In this section, the relationship between energy use and the conditions associated with IAP and respiratory health in children under age five are explored. This group was selected because the literature shows that children of this age are most vulnerable to ARI, but also because the two national surveys limit their measurement of respiratory illness to infants and young children.

Table 2.6 Combination of Fuels and Kitchen Facilities in Guatemalan Homes

percent

Fuel and kitchen combination	Type of fuel	Type of kitchen	Region								
			Metropolitan	North	Northeast	Southeast	Central	Southwest	Northwest	Petén	Total
Urban											
1. Worst	Dirty	Shared	2.2	10.6	3.5	6.2	10.0	2.1	13.5	9.9	4.4
2.	Mixed	Shared	18.9	6.3	16.0	12.3	24.0	9.9	13.2	11.1	16.7
3.	Dirty	Exclusive	2.7	29.1	15.8	19.5	17.6	20.7	22.4	27.5	11.4
4.	Mixed	Exclusive	24.9	30.2	24.4	31.1	24.4	35.6	32.1	28.9	27.5
5. Best	Clean	Outdoors	51.3	23.8	40.4	30.8	24.0	31.7	18.7	22.6	40.1
Rural											
1. Worst	Dirty	Shared	12.6	38.9	14.8	7.8	30.2	16.0	24.8	19.5	20.1
2.	Mixed	Shared	7.3	1.2	12.0	4.7	11.1	13.4	9.9	0.8	9.4
3.	Dirty	Exclusive	41.9	51.7	38.7	61.5	31.1	44.9	52.8	68.2	47.3
4.	Mixed	Exclusive	29.9	6.4	24.8	18.0	16.8	20.6	11.1	6.2	17.4
5. Best	Clean	Outdoors	8.3	1.9	9.6	8.1	10.9	5.1	1.4	5.2	5.8
Total											
1. Worst	Dirty	Shared	3.5	33.7	11.7	7.4	20.7	11.9	22.7	16.5	13.3
2.	Mixed	Shared	17.4	2.1	13.1	6.6	17.1	12.4	10.6	4.1	12.5
3.	Dirty	Exclusive	7.7	47.5	32.3	51.1	24.8	37.8	47.1	55.3	31.7
4.	Mixed	Exclusive	25.5	10.8	24.7	21.2	20.3	25.0	15.1	13.4	21.8
5. Best	Clean	Outdoors	45.8	5.9	18.1	13.7	17.1	12.9	4.6	10.7	20.7
Total			100	100	100	100	100	100	100	100	100

Source: LSMS (World Bank/INE/UN 2000).

Note: Rankings (worst to best) are based on exposure to IAP. When clean fuels are used, there are negligible or no emissions, so they do not matter. When cooking outdoors, exposure to IAP is considered negligible, regardless of the fuel used.

The two infant health issues that can be addressed using these national surveys are infant morbidity and mortality. Only the DHS study has information on mortality of children younger than age five, but out of a total of 4,435 children up to age five, only 227 (5.1 percent) were reported to have died. It was impossible to use these data to examine the relationship between household characteristics and the infant mortality rate. The LSMS likewise does not account for deceased children. Both surveys do, however, provide information on children's respiratory illness: The DHS and LSMS asked the parents and guardians whether their children had experienced respiratory illness during the previous two weeks and one month, respectively. Therefore, in this section the relationship between children's respiratory illness and factors related to IAP are examined.

Evidence from the DHS Study

The DHS collected information on both respiratory illness and the types of fuels used and the cooking environment in the home. Questions were asked of the guardian regarding any illnesses suffered by children in the house during the previous two weeks. One category of illness noted was the respiratory problem of a cough and shortness of breath; another was for the same symptoms but accompanied by fever. Combining this information with the information on household characteristics of fuel use and type of kitchen can indicate whether the presence of smoke in the household has an impact on children's health.

The findings from this study are consistent with some of the recent literature on IAP and health. The most serious ARI symptoms were present in 15 percent of children living in homes cooking with fuelwood and in 11 percent of children living in homes using clean fuels (table 2.7). A separate room for cooking seems significant for the prevention of ARI symptoms: About 18 percent of children in homes with common cooking and sleeping or living quarters have serious symptoms, compared to 13 percent of children living in homes with a separate kitchen. Combining these two findings, homes that use biomass fuels and that have a shared-use kitchen have a serious-infection rate of 19 percent, compared to just 11 percent of households that use LPG. Conversely, the highest proportion of children with no symptoms is 74 percent of those living in households using LPG, compared to 65 percent of children in households that use biomass in a common room. It would also appear that having a separate kitchen combined with a chimney has almost as much impact as using LPG.

The group of households that use LPG includes a greater proportion of urban, wealthy households than the group that uses biomass. Poor diet, poor sanitation, and many other factors may be contributing to these findings. Nonetheless, it is likely that cooking smoke has at least a contributory effect on the distribution of respiratory illness.

Table 2.7 Respiratory Symptoms in Children by Fuel and Cooking Space from 1998–1999 DHS

percent

Part A Fuel type and cooking areas

	Fuel		Cooking area		
	Biomass	*LPG*	*No kitchen*	*Kitchen*	*Total*
No symptoms	68	74	65	71	69
Cough and breath shortness	16	15	17	16	16
Cough, breath shortness, and fever	15	11	18	13	14
Total	100	100	100	100	100
Total children (cases)	3,303	769	1,012	2,074	4,086

Part B Fuel type combined with cooking areas

	Biomass, no kitchen, no chimney	*Biomass, kitchen, no chimney*	*Biomass, kitchen, chimney*	*LPG*	*Total*
No symptoms	65	69	72	74	69
Cough and breath shortness	16	17	14	15	16
Cough, breath shortness, and fever	19	14	14	11	15
Total	100	100	100	100	100
Total children (cases)	773	1,987	487	769	4,016

Source: DHS (Macro International 1999).

24

Evidence from the LSMS Study

The measure of respiratory illness provided by the LSMS data is less satisfactory than that made possible by the DHS. In the LSMS study, the single question asked about respiratory illness covers a spectrum of symptoms that, while certainly referring to respiratory illnesses, cannot be unequivocally elevated to ARI. Furthermore, the reference period is one full month, which also poses problems of correct recall by respondents. The longer recall period does, however, have the advantage of returning a higher proportion of respondents displaying some kind of symptoms. The survey sample also is larger, including 6,074 children under age five.

Once again, the findings presented in table 2.8 merely indicate association, and other factors such as income class, access to health facilities, and sanitary conditions may be contributing to these findings. There seems, nonetheless, to be a significant association between respiratory symptoms and the type of fuel used in the home and whether there is a separate kitchen for cooking. Generally, in homes using fuelwood alone or in combination with petroleum fuels, the level of respiratory illness symptoms in children was between 45 percent and 51 percent. By contrast, for homes using mainly petroleum fuels such as LPG or in which there is no cooking, the incidence of symptoms of respiratory illness was between 40 percent and 42 percent. It would seem,

Table 2.8 Respiratory Symptoms in Children by Fuel and Cooking Space from 2000 LSMS
percent

	Fuel			
Part A: Fuel type	Fuelwood only	Mix of fuelwood, LPG, and other	Clean only (mainly LPG)	Total
No symptoms	52	54	60	53
Respiratory illness	48	46	40	47
Total	100	100	100	100
Total children (cases)	3,631	1,769	649	6,049

	Fuel and room for cooking					
Part B: Fuel type and cooking area	Biomass, no kitchen	Mixed, no kitchen	Biomass, kitchen	Mixed, kitchen	LPG, kitchen	Total
No symptoms	50	47	53	57	58	53
Respiratory illness	50	53	47	43	42	47
Total	100	100	100	100	100	100
Total children (cases)	1,167	661	2,314	1,069	841	6,052

Source: LSMS (World Bank/INE/UN 2000).

therefore, that the availability of a kitchen exclusively for cooking decreases the incidence of respiratory illness, but this finding is also related to whether fuelwood is used in conjunction with clean fuels or alone.

The overall indications of the LSMS data are similar to those of the DHS. Reductions in respiratory illness symptoms are associated both with the use of petroleum fuels and with the use of a separate room for cooking. Disentangling some of the causal associations with respiratory illness that are due to income, sanitary conditions, drinking water, and other factors is still required.

A study by Martinez Cuellar (2003) also used the LSMS data to assess whether such factors as the use of a chimney or the use of wood are related to respiratory illness in children. The results of this work highlight how difficult it is to sort out causes and effects.[2] The findings indicate that the use of wood for cooking increases the incidence of respiratory illness among children by about 35 percent, and that the use of a chimney for cooking reduces the incidence by about 45 percent. The conclusion of the Martinez Cuellar study is that even after controlling for other important factors there is a relationship between clean air in the home and a reduction of children's respiratory illness.However, given the difficulties of attributing causality with cross-sectional health data, we would still have to to conclude that the findings to date are inconclusive; they do, however, represent preliminary steps in the complex process of linking IAP and health.

Conclusion

A growing body of work has detected alarmingly high levels of IAP in homes that use traditional solid fuels. A number of studies in Guatemala have confirmed the high exposure to toxic pollutants from fuelwood combustion that women and children endure. The literature also points to the strong association between IAP and health conditions, particularly among children in their first few years of life. This book draws upon the 1998–1999 DHS and the 2000 LSMS databases for Guatemala to verify whether large national surveys can broaden to the national level the evidence already discerned by surveys at the village, household, and cookstove levels in Guatemala's highlands. The results of this work have shown that there is evidence of a relationship between both infant mortality and ARI and the use of wood without chimneys for cooking.

Several limitations were confronted in the analysis of both surveys. First, both the DHS and LSMS lack information directly related to the subject. The DHS lacks direct information on household income, ARI symptoms, and women's respiratory illness. The LSMS lacks clarity on ARI symptoms and on the relative use of fuels in households that use more than one fuel. For comparative international analysis it is interesting to use these standardized databases, but of their thousands of variables there are disappointingly few that are directly pertinent to the type of analysis desired. As IAP becomes a more visible issue, it would be helpful to incorporate into the DHS and LSMS questionnaires a specific module or set of questions related to health and kitchen smoke: for example, questions on the size and ventilation conditions of the kitchen, on the amount of exposure to smoke per typical day, and on the precise symptoms of ARI, both for children and women.

The combined evidence from health and IAP studies and national survey analysis indicates an association between fuelwood smoke and infant respiratory illness in Guatemala. However, ambiguity remains. Our level of knowledge of the phenomenon in this country must be improved on the basis of more specific surveys and measurements, using representative sampling techniques at the national level, if we are to design and substantiate public policies geared toward mitigating the effects of IAP on human health. This would include the development and use of specific questions or modules in future LSMSs and DHSs to pinpoint ARI symptoms in children and adults, and to quantify fuel and kitchen use patterns, ventilation, and exposure times to fuelwood smoke. The development of self-standing, national-scale survey and measurement instruments may be advisable, with sampling techniques, questionnaires, and the use of technologies designed specifically to investigate energy-pollution-health interactions. For public policy purposes, a nexus could be developed between the epidemiological and econometric approaches to analyze the effects of IAP on human health.

Cooking patterns in Guatemala's urban areas, and most notably in the metropolitan area, seem to have shifted radically from fuelwood use to LPG. While there has been some change in rural areas also, traditional fuelwood use remains predominant. Consumer choice is not a clear-cut question of either fuelwood or LPG, however: There is strong evidence, particularly in the LSMS, that a large proportion of households combine the use of both clean and polluting fuels. Thus, it will become increasingly difficult to determine from the available data the levels of the impacts of IAP on human health.

Notes

1. The correlation between income per person and consumer expenditure per person is 0.613. The asset index (0.471) is similar to that of the DHS survey, which means that there is an R square of 0.38 and 0.22 respectively. This is based on 7,275 cases and the coefficients are significant at the 0.001 level. The correlation between the asset index and expenditure per person in the family is 0.529, with an R square of 0.28.

2. The model used estimates whether the household choice of wood or use of a chimney relates to the health of children in the family. The results suggest that there is a significant relationship between the choice of fuels and stove and the incidence of respiratory illness among children in the family.

3
Estimating Health Impacts

This chapter presents estimates of the health impacts of indoor air pollution (IAP) in Guatemala. The purpose of these estimates is to provide an indication of the potential severity of the problem for policy makers. This chapter specifically focuses on estimating the health impacts of traditional fuel use in the rural areas of the Guatemalan highlands, where the impact is potentially most severe. In the northwest and southwest of Guatemala, approximately two-thirds of households use wood fires, without chimneys, for heating and cooking. The associated levels of PM_{10} (particulate matter with an aerodynamic diameter less than 10 microns) inside these houses are in excess of 1,000 $\mu g/m^3$. The estimates focus on the reduction in morbidity and mortality associated with acute lower respiratory infection (ALRI) for children under age five living in households that use open fires. Dose-response functions from the international epidemiological literature are used to predict the reductions in mortality and morbidity if PM_{10} levels were to be lowered to less than 200 $\mu g/m^3$. This level could, in theory at least, be achieved by a well-maintained improved stove.

The following sections provide a brief description of the scope of this chapter, examine the characteristics of IAP in the Guatemalan highlands that are used in estimating the health impacts of IAP, and describe in greater detail the methodology used to estimate the health impacts of IAP.

Scope of the Study

The effects of indoor air pollution are vast. This particular study restricts its scope to the effects of IAP with respect to acute lower respiratory infections in children under age five in the Guatemalan highlands.

Target Health Outcome: Acute Lower Respiratory Infection

For practical reasons, this chapter focuses on the effects of IAP on ALRI. According to Von Schirnding and others (2001, p. 6):

> There is consistent evidence that exposure to biomass smoke increases the risk of a range of common and serious diseases of both children and adults. Chief amongst these are acute lower respiratory infections (ALRIs) in childhood, particularly pneumonia.

The health impacts of IAP are not limited to ALRI. Smith (2000) divides the evidence on the health effects of IAP into three classes: strong, moderate, and suggestive, as follows: He cites strong evidence for acute respiratory infection (ARI) in children under age five, for chronic obstructive pulmonary disease (COPD) in women, and for lung cancer in women. The epidemiological literature linking IAP to COPD in women is limited in comparison to the literature linking IAP to ARI in children. Lung cancer in women is a well-demonstrated outcome of cooking with open coal stoves in China, but coal is not commonly used as cooking fuel in the Guatemalan highlands. Based on these observations, this chapter estimates the health impacts only for ARI in children under age five. Because the health effects in women are ignored, these estimates constitute a lower bound to the health benefits of reducing IAP.

Smith classifies as moderate the evidence regarding a relationship between solid fuel use and other health outcomes such as cataracts and blindness, tuberculosis, asthma, and adverse pregnancy outcomes. He cites evidence of IAP causing heart disease in women as suggestive only, because there do not appear to be any studies of heart disease related to indoor biomass use in developing countries.

ARI is among the class of disease risks with strong evidence of a relationship with IAP. The definition used for ARI is as follows (Smith and others 2000, p. 520):

> . . . it comprises a set of clinical conditions of various etiologies and severities that are generally divided into two main forms: upper respiratory tract infections (URIs) and lower respiratory tract infections (ALRIs). . . . WHO defines URI to include any combination of the following symptoms: cough with or without fever, blocked or runny nose, sore throat, and/or ear discharge. . . . ALRI includes severe ARI involving infection of the lungs, with pneumonia being the most serious form. . . . Clinical signs of ALRI include any of the above symptoms of URI with the addition of rapid breathing and/or chest indrawing and/or stridor.

Target Age Group: Children under Age Five

This chapter concentrates on children under age five, as they are at highest risk of contracting acute respiratory diseases thought to be linked to IAP. ARI is the most common cause of illness in children and the leading cause worldwide of death in children under age five. As noted by Smith (2000, p. 518), "among children under five years of age, 3 to 5 million deaths annually have been attributed to ARI, of which 75 percent are from pneumonia." In addition, in houses where biomass fuels are used, children under five are likely to be more exposed to air pollution than older children.

Children under five spend more time at home with their mothers and thus receive higher exposures than older children, who may spend much time away from the household. The epidemiological literature relating IAP to respiratory illness is also larger for children under age five than it is for other age groups. Due to these factors, this chapter focuses entirely on the effects of IAP on children under age five.

Target Area: Guatemalan Highlands

The population studied consists of households in the rural highlands of Guatemala, defined as the southwest (SW) and northwest (NW) regions of the country. Approximately two-thirds of these households rely on open wood fires for heating and cooking, often in houses where ventilation is poor. Children in these households are exposed to high levels of particulate matter. Approximately one-quarter of the households use improved stoves, which should reduce indoor particulate concentrations. The main objective of the chapter is to estimate how many fewer fatal and nonfatal cases of ALRI would result if households that currently use open fires were to switch to improved stoves.

Information on fuel use in Guatemala is based on two databases that were designed to be representative at the national and regional levels: the 1998–1999 Demographic and Health Survey (DHS) (Macro International 1999) and the 2000 Living Standards Measurement Study (LSMS) (World Bank/INE/UN 2000).

Indoor Air Pollution in the Guatemalan Highlands

This section analyzes two main determinants of individual exposure to IAP: the type of fuel used for cooking, and the related ambient levels of particulate matter. The implied individual exposure to IAP will, in turn, be used to estimate the health impacts of IAP.

Types of Fuels Used for Cooking

The DHS and LSMS provide information on fuels used for cooking, on the existence of a separate room (kitchen) for cooking, and on the use of chimneys. However, these surveys do not provide direct information on indoor concentrations of particulate matter (PM) or on personal exposures to PM. Table 3.1 summarizes the indirect evidence of exposure to IAP that is available from the DHS. The DHS sample was designed to be representative at the national and regional levels. Of the 5,587 households in the sample, 1,152 were in rural areas in the SW region and 703 in rural areas in the NW region of Guatemala.

Table 3.1 Percentage of Rural Households Using Fuelwood, Conditional on House Characteristics

Fuel	Separate kitchen	Chimney in kitchen	Southwest	Northwest
Fuelwood	no	no	12.1	18.1
Fuelwood	yes	no	55.3	48.4
Fuelwood	yes	yes	22.6	29.7
Clean Fuel			10.1	3.9
			100	100

Source: Torres 2002.

Note: Percentages may not add to 100 due to rounding.

Table 3.1 shows that wood is the main cooking fuel in the Guatemalan highlands. Wood is used by a total of 89.9 percent of rural households in the SW and 96.1 percent in the NW. The majority of households—67.3 percent of households in the SW and 66.5 percent in the NW—burn wood in open fires, without a chimney. Approximately one-quarter of households burn wood in a stove with a chimney. Clean fuel (kerosene, liquefied petroleum gas [LPG], and electricity) is used by 10.1 percent of rural households in the SW region and by 3.9 percent in the NW region. The LSMS supports the same general patterns, but provides complementary information: According to the LSMS, charcoal is not commonly used in rural areas of Guatemala, as only 3.4 percent of households use it for cooking.

In addition to the DHS and LSMS, studies providing detailed information regarding biomass usage in Guatemala have been undertaken in rural villages in the western highlands of the country, especially in the area of Quetzaltenango.[1] Quetzaltenango is a mountainous region with altitudes in the range of 2,500–2,800 meters. An initial survey in Los Romeros, Quetzaltenango, indicated that "70 percent of the households have only open fires for cooking, 25 percent have some form of improved wood-burning stoves, and 5 percent have gas stoves" McCracken and others (1999, p. 122).

Other information on cooking fuel use for the area can be found in the study by Albalak and others (2001, p. 2,651), which states that "as of September 1998, 49 percent of the 867 households in La Victoria [Quetzaltenango] used a traditional open firewood cookstove for all their cooking needs. Thirty-one percent used the *plancha* exclusively, and 10 percent used an LPG/open fire combination." These results are broadly consistent with the DHS survey results reported in table 3.1.

Indoor concentrations of PM$_{10}$. Ambient concentrations of particulate matter inside houses differ depending on the type of cooking fuel used, whether it is burned in a stove or open fire, and whether a chimney is used. Table 3.2 summarizes the available information on ambient IAP concentrations in the Guatemalan highlands, measured as particulate matter monitored in the kitchen area. The study by Naeher, Leaderer, and Smith (2000), which was conducted during the fall, selected three houses in which open fires were used for cooking and measured indoor PM concentrations ($PM_{2.5}$, PM_{10}, and total suspended particles) in these houses when an open fire was used, when the open fire was replaced by a *plancha*, and when the open fire was replaced by a gas stove. The study attached personal monitors to the mother and child for 12 hours. Because new *planchas* were introduced solely for the study, the results cannot be considered representative of normal operating conditions.

The study by Albalak and others (2001) monitored 30 households six times during the year (between December and July), with one-third of the households using each cooking type (LPG, *plancha*, open fire). The authors noted that the *planchas* were in relatively good condition, but were not new, nor did they appear to have been *planchas mejoradas*.[2] Naeher and others (1999) carried out a cross-sectional study in which measurements of $PM_{2.5}$ (particulate matter with an aerodynamic diameter less than 2.5 microns) were reported for both *planchas* already in place and open fires. The study by McCracken and others (1999) measured 24-hour average $PM_{2.5}$ concentrations in 45 homes over a period of five months (six observations per house), with the sample evenly divided between households using an open fire for cooking, households using LPG, and households using an improved *plancha* (*plancha mejorada*). Smith and others (1993) measured concentrations inside 60 homes, 23 of which used open fires, 25 of which used *planchas*, and 12 of which used LPG for cooking.

In all the studies in table 3.2, kitchen PM concentrations (24-hour average) were significantly higher when an open wood fire was used for cooking than when a *plancha* was used. Average PM_{10} concentrations reported by Smith and others (1993) with an open wood fire were 1,210 $\mu g/m^3$. This is much higher than the concentration of 717.1 $\mu g/m^3$ reported by Naeher, Leaderer, and Smith (2000). However, the study by Naeher, Leaderer, and Smith was conducted in the fall, when temperatures are higher than in the winter months and when home heating requirements consequently may be lower. Four of the studies in table 3.2 reported $PM_{2.5}$ concentrations. Albalak and others (2001) reported the highest average 24-hour concentrations: 1,930 $\mu g/m^3$. McCracken and others (1999) reported an average 24-hour $PM_{2.5}$ concentration of 1,102 $\mu g/m^3$. The figures for $PM_{2.5}$ and PM_{10} in the studies by Naeher and others (1999) and Naeher, Leaderer, and Smith (2000) are lower than for the other studies.

By averaging the $PM_{2.5}$ concentrations in table 3.2, weighting each by the number of observations reported in the study, the mean concentration is revealed to be 1,325 $\mu g/m^3$. Using the ratio of PM_{10} to $PM_{2.5}$ for open fire reported by Naeher, Leaderer, and Smith (2000)—that is, 717.1 to 527.9—a

Table 3.2 Personal and Daily Average Kitchen Measurements of Particulate Matter in the Guatemalan Highlands

		Daily average concentrations in kitchen area						Personal monitoring	
Stove condition		Data for PM$_{2.5}$ (Naeher, Leaderer, and Smith 2000) μg/m³	Data for PM$_{10}$ (Naeher, Leaderer, and Smith 2000) μg/m³	Data for PM$_{2.5}$ (Albalak and others 2001)[a] μg/m³	Data for PM$_{2.5}$ (Naeher and others 1999) μg/m³	Data for PM$_{2.5}$ (McCracken and others 1999) μg/m³	Data for PM$_{10}$ (Smith and others 1993) μg/m³	Data for PM$_{2.5}$ (Naeher, Leaderer, and Smith 2000) μg/m³ child	Data for PM$_{2.5}$ (Naeher, Leaderer, and Smith 2000) μg/m³ mother
Background	Average	56.2	183.9	174.1					
	Std. dev.	17.6	134.6	113					
	Sample size	9	8	9					
LPG stove	Average	56.8	210.2	217.7				148.5	135.6
	Std. dev.	19	100.3	88.1				68.5	117
	Sample size	9	9	9				3	3
Comal LPG (real conditions with open fire)	Average					790			
	Std. dev.					654			
	Sample size					60			
Plancha mejorada	Average					180			
	Std. dev.					107			
	Sample size					60			
Plancha (in good condition)	Average	96.5	186.3	330				169.7	257.2
	Std. dev.	66.5	89.5	220				153.6	75.4
	Sample size	9	9	59				3	3
Plancha (real conditions)	Average				152		520		
	Std. dev.				120		572		
	Sample size				26		25		
Open fire	Average	527.9	717.1	1,930	868	1,102	1,210	279.1	481.2
	Std. dev.	248.5	284.6	1,280	520	606	726	19.5	194.4
	Sample size	9	9	58	17	60	23	2	3

Sources: Albalak and others 2001; McCracken and others 1999; Naeher and others 1999; Naeher, Leaderer, and Smith 2000; Smith and others 1993.

a. Albalak and others (2001) refer to particles measured as PM$_{3.5}$, because the SKC (name of manufacturer's model) monitors used in the study were run at a flow rate of 2 liters per minute to avoid saturating the filters. This is the same flow rate at which the monitors were run by McCracken and others (1999), who refer to measuring PM$_{2.5}$. The Albalak and others measurements are therefore referred to as measurements of PM$_{2.5}$.

33

24-hour average PM_{10} concentration of approximately 1,800 $\mu g/m^3$ is obtained.

Ambient levels of PM when a *plancha* is used depend on how the stove is maintained. Table 3.2 shows that concentrations of $PM_{2.5}$ and PM_{10} of less than 200 $\mu g/m^3$ can be achieved with a well-maintained *plancha*. Under actual conditions of use, the emissions from a *plancha* may be considerably higher. The study by Smith and others (1993) indicates that 24-hour concentrations of 520 $\mu g/m^3$ of PM_{10} can be achieved for a *plancha*. Using the ratio of $PM_{2.5}$ to PM_{10} (186.3 to 96.5) reported by Naeher, Leaderer, and Smith (2000), the $PM_{2.5}$ concentration associated with the *plancha* in the study by Smith and others (1993) would be approximately 1,004 $\mu g/m^3$.

Individual exposure estimation. Predicting cases of ALRI associated with IAP requires that the personal exposure to PM_{10} of children in the Guatemalan highlands be estimated. For the purposes of this study, the challenge inherent in making such predictions on the basis of the average kitchen concentrations reported in table 3.2 lies in determining how long children are exposed to these concentrations. One approach is to use the ratio of a child's personal exposure to average kitchen concentrations in a household with an open fire, as reported in Naeher, Leaderer, and Smith (2000). This ratio (0.53), when applied to the estimated 24-hour PM_{10} kitchen concentration of 1,800 $\mu g/m^3$ in households with open fires, suggests a personal PM_{10} exposure of 954 $\mu g/m^3$ (24-hour average). The Naeher, Leaderer, and Smith results are, however, based on only two observations.

Ezzati, Saleh, and Kammen (2000), in their study of exposure to PM_{10} in villages in Kenya, suggest that average indoor concentrations are a good proxy for the personal exposure of children under age five, suggesting a personal PM_{10} exposure for such children in homes with open fires of 1,800 $\mu g/m^3$ (24-hour average). In view of the fact that children in Kenya are not carried on their mother's back, as they are in Guatemala, the estimate of exposure levels in Guatemala could be higher.

Estimation of Health Impacts of IAP

Estimating the health impacts of exposure to IAP requires dose-response (or concentration-response) information from the epidemiological litera-ture relating ALRI to exposure to IAP. A review article by Smith and others (2000) summarizes 13 studies conducted in developing countries that relate IAP to ALRI in children.[3] Three of the studies examine the impact of IAP on mortality; the others examine the impact of IAP on morbidity.

The main difficulties in establishing a relationship between ALRI and IAP lie in measuring exposure to IAP and in controlling for confounding factors, that is, variables that are correlated with the use of biomass fuels that may also contribute to ALRI. In all but one of the studies reviewed by Smith and others (2000), exposure to IAP is measured by a qualitative index; for example, an indicator variable = 1 if biomass fuel is used for cooking, or an indicator variable = 1 if the child is carried on the mother's back during cooking. The only study conducted in a developing country that has carefully attempted to measure indoor air concentrations and personal exposures is Ezzati and Kammen (2001a), which is discussed in more detail below.

Controlling for confounding variables is especially important in IAP studies. The use of biomass for cooking is likely to be inversely correlated with income, access to health care, and good nutrition, all of which could affect the incidence of ALRI. A study that fails to control for these factors may simply demonstrate that poor children are more likely to contract (and die from) ALRI than are children who are better off. Five of the studies reviewed by Smith and others (2000) make no attempt to adjust for confounders. Other studies attempt variously to control for number of siblings, crowding, birthweight, and economic status. As table 3A.1 in the annex to this chapter indicates, the studies with the largest odds ratios are those that fail to control for confounders.

The World Health Organization, when computing the global burden of disease associated with IAP, relied on an odds ratio for ALRI morbidity and mortality associated with IAP of 2.3 [95 percent CI (confidence interval): 1.9, 2.7] (WHO 2002). This was based on a meta-analysis of the studies reported in Smith and others (2000). The assumption that an odds ratio based primarily on studies of the impact of IAP on morbidity should apply equally to mortality is questionable. In particular, it assumes that IAP has no impact on the case fatality rate associated with ALRI. There are, however, an insufficient number of case-fatality studies in the literature to permit estimation of an odds ratio for mortality.

In the study in this book, calculation of the impacts of exposure to IAP in the Guatemalan highlands is based solely on the work by Ezzati and Kammen (2001a), which is the only study to date to associate the incidence of respiratory illness to personal measurements of exposure to PM_{10}. The study was carried out in the Laikipia district of central Kenya, a mountainous region in which the rate of under-five child mortality is comparable to that in the Guatemalan highlands.[4] Members of 55 households were followed for two years, receiving biweekly and then weekly visits from a nurse to diagnose cases of ARI. A measure of personal exposure to PM_{10} was constructed for each household member, based on a sample of measurements inside each house and combined with information on the length of time spent in various microenvironments by each household member.

Table 3.3 summarizes the odds ratios reported in Ezzati and Kammen (2001a) for logistic regression models to explain the incidence of ARI and

Table 3.3 Adjusted Odds Ratios for ARI and ALRI in Children under Age Five Estimated with a Logistic Model

	ARI (n = 93)		ALRI (n = 93)	
Factor	Odds ratio (95% CI)	p statistic	Odds ratio (95% CI)	p statistic
PM exposure ($\mu g/m^3$)				
<200	1.00	—	1.00	—
200–500	2.42 (1.53–3.83)	0.001*	1.48 (0.83–2.63)	0.18*
500–1,000	2.15 (1.30–3.56)	0.003*	1.40 (0.74–2.67)	0.30*
1,000–2,000	4.30 (2.63–7.04)	0.001*	2.33 (1.23–4.38)	0.01*
2,000–3,500	4.72 (2.82–7.88)	0.001*	1.93 (0.99–3.78)	0.05*
2,000–4,000	—	—	—	—
>3,500	6.73 (3.75–12.06)	0.001*	2.93 (1.34–6.39)	0.007*
4,000–7,000	—	—	—	—
>7,000	—	—	—	—
Female	0.99 (0.83–1.17)	0.88	0.84 (0.65–1.10)	0.21
Age+	0.88 (0.83–0.94)	0.001	0.76 (0.70–0.84)	0.001
Smoking	—	—	—	—
Village type++	1.29 (0.99–1.67)	0.06	1.18 (0.79–1.77)	0.41
Number of people in house+	1.00 (0.95–1.05)	0.99	0.98 (0.91–1.06)	0.70

Source: Ezzati and Kammen 2001a.

Notes: * Jointly significant ($p < 0.01$).
+ Odds ratio of illness with every additional year of age/extra person in house.
++ Cattle compound or maintenance compound.

ALRI among children under age five. The distribution of the 93 children, according to their category of exposure, is as follows:

- 7 children with an average daily exposure <200 $\mu g/m^3$
- 20 children with an average daily exposure of 200–500 $\mu g/m^3$
- 20 children with an average daily exposure of 500–1,000 $\mu g/m^3$
- 21 children with an average daily exposure of 1,000–2,000 $\mu g/m^3$
- 20 children with an average daily exposure of 2,000–3500 $\mu g/m^3$
- 5 children with an average daily exposure >3,500 $\mu g/m^3$

As indicated in table 3.3, the models control for household size and village type, as well as for age and sex.

Focusing on ALRI, the odds ratio for exposures of 1,000–2,000 $\mu g/m^3$ is significantly different from zero at the 0.009 level; however, the odds ratios for lower exposures are not significant at conventional levels. The small number of controls in the reference exposure category (<200 $\mu g/m^3$), together with the lack of statistical significance of exposure of 200–500 $\mu g/m^3$, suggests that combining the lowest two categories might produce different results.[5]

Calculation of ALRI Associated with IAP in Guatemala

As indicated in the previous section, this study assumes that children in households using open fires fall in the exposure range of 1,000–2,000 $\mu g/m^3$, which is associated with an odds ratio of 2.33 for ALRI [95 percent CI: 1.23, 4.38], compared with exposures of <200 $\mu g/m^3$. Therefore, this odds ratio was used to calculate cases of excess morbidity and mortality associated with ALRI for children in households where open fires are used. The estimates of excess morbidity and mortality shown in table 3.4 represent how many fewer cases of ALRI would be achieved if exposure levels for these children were to be reduced to less than 200 $\mu g/m^3$, a level that, in theory, could be achieved by a well-maintained *plancha* or by reliance on a gas stove for heating and cooking. To the extent that there are benefits from reducing the exposures of children in households with *planchas* who fall in the exposure range between 1,000 $\mu g/m^3$ of PM_{10} and 200 $\mu g/m^3$, these calculations understate the burden of ALRI associated with IAP in the Guatemalan highlands.

Cases of Excess Morbidity

The numbers of children under age five in the different *departamentos* of the Guatemalan highlands were obtained from the 1994 National Population Census (INE 1994) as shown in table 3.5. It is assumed, following table 3.1, that 67.3 percent of the children in the SW region and 66.5 percent in the NW region lived in households where open fires were used for cooking; 22.6 percent in the SW and 29.7 percent in the NW lived in households where *planchas* were used for cooking; and 10.1 percent in the SW and 3.9 percent in the NW lived in households where clean fuels were used for cooking. The incidence rates for ALRI in each *departamento* are also presented in table 3.5. Due to the tendency by many *departamentos* for underreporting, these figures may be lower than the true incidence rates. No attempt is made in the subsequent calculation to adjust for this possible underreporting.

The calculation of cases of excess morbidity due to IAP exposure (relative to the baseline of <200 $\mu g/m^3$ PM_{10}) is as follows: Each ALRI incidence rate in table 3.5 represents a weighted average of the incidence rate for children not exposed to IAP (m) and the incidence rate for exposed children—2.33 times m.[6] Once m is calculated, the excess incidence rate ($2.33m - m$) is

Table 3.4 Excess Cases of ALRI Morbidity and Mortality in the Guatemalan Highlands Associated with IAP

Departamento	Excess cases of ALRI morbidity caused by IAP, children exposed to open fire OR 95% CI = [1.23–4.38] reduction = 19% to 77%			Age-specific 0–4 mortality rate[a] (per 1,000)	Percentage of deaths due to pneumonia[b]	Estimated age-specific 0–4 mortality rate due to ALRI (per 1,000)	Excess cases of ALRI mortality caused by IAP, children exposed to open fire OR 95% CI = [1.23–4.38] reduction = 19% to 77%		
Odds Ratio	1.23	2.33	4.38				1.23	2.33	4.38
Solola	711	2,506	3,685	13.55	24.61	3.33	16	58	85
Totonicapan	782	2,755	4,052	16.54	34.89	5.77	43	152	224
Quetzaltenango	525	1,851	2,722	13.32	30.51	4.06	40	141	207
Suchitepequez	575	2,026	2,979	11.90	16.09	1.91	13	44	65
Retalhuleu	308	1,086	1,597	11.82	17.30	2.05	8	29	43
San Marcos	1,754	6,179	9,088	9.63	36.44	3.51	62	219	323
Huehuetenango	1,349	4,772	7,037	8.13	36.85	3.00	54	193	284
Quiche	837	2,961	4,366	12.18	33.85	4.12	50	175	258
Total	6,841	24,135	35,526				288	1,014	1,493

Source: Indicadores Básicos de Salud en Guatemala 2001, Ministerio de Salud Publica y Asistencia Social, Guatemala.

OR = odds ratio.

a. Age-specific 0–4 mortality rate was calculated as a weighted average from data on infant mortality and mortality between ages one and four.
b. Corresponds to the percentage of deaths during the first year of life caused by pneumonia.

Table 3.5 Number of Children under Age Five and ALRI Incidence Rates

Departamento	Region	Children under age five	Number of children in the high exposure range (Open fire)	Number of children in the medium exposure range (Plancha)	Number of children in the low exposure range	ALRI rate of incidence (per 10,000 under age five)
Percentage of children in each range of exposure	SW		67.3	22.6	10.1	
	NW		66.5	29.7	3.9	
Solola	SW	36,580	24,624	8,255	3,701	1,450
Totonicapan	SW	55,810	37,569	12,595	5,646	1,045
Quetzaltenango	SW	73,502	49,478	16,588	7,436	533
Suchitepequez	SW	48,948	32,950	11,047	4,952	876
Retalhuleu	SW	30,160	20,302	6,807	3,051	762
San Marcos	SW	132,257	89,029	29,848	13,380	989
Huehuetenango	NW	136,940	90,999	40,640	5,301	743
Quiche	NW	90,696	60,269	26,916	3,511	696
Total		604,893	405,219	152,696	46,978	

Source: Vigilancia Epidemiológica, Ministerio de Salud Pública y Asistencia Social, Guatemala.

Note: Totals may not be exact due to rounding.

then multiplied by the number of children in each *departamento* living in households with open fires. The results show a total of 24,135 excess cases of ALRI morbidity attributed to IAP, as presented in table 3.4.

Cases of Excess Mortality

The number of children dying from ALRI can be expressed as:

$$N*(\text{ALRI cases}/10,000)*\text{case fatality rate}$$
$$= N*(\text{deaths due to ALRI}/10,000)$$

where N represents the number of children in a particular group. Assuming that the case fatality rate remains unaffected by the intervention program to reduce IAP, it follows from the equation that the percentage reduction in ALRI cases must equal the percentage reduction in deaths due to ALRI. An odds ratio of 2.33 implies a 57.1 percent reduction in the death rate due to ALRI.

Table 3.4 calculates the expected reduction in deaths due to ALRI for each *departamento*. The death rate due to ALRI is approximated by multiplying the age-specific, age 0–4 mortality rate for each *departamento* by the percentage of deaths due to pneumonia during the first year of life. The age-specific 0–4 death rate due to ALRI is used to calculate the death rate for children exposed to IAP assuming that their death rate is 2.33 times the death rate of children who are not exposed. This is then multiplied by the number of children exposed to open fires (shown in table 3.5) to calculate the expected number of children under age five in homes with open fires who die annually from ALRI. For the NW and SW regions combined, this figure is 1,774. The estimated number of excess ALRI mortality cases (relative to a baseline of $<200 \ \mu g/m^3 \ PM_{10}$) is 57.1 percent of 1,774, or 1,014 deaths. Figures corresponding to a 95 percent confidence interval are also presented in the table.

An immediate implication of the results in table 3.4 is that the case fatality rate—the number of excess deaths due to ALRI divided by the number of excess cases—varies greatly by *departamento*. Focusing on the ratio of point estimates, the case fatality rates implied by table 3.4 range from 0.022 to 0.076. These rates are correlated with the percentage of the population in poverty in each *departamento*.[7]

Conclusions

This chapter estimates the magnitude of health damages associated with IAP to children under age five in the Guatemalan highlands. For children living in homes in which open fires are used for heating and cooking, we calculate that there are approximately 24,000 cases of ALRI [95 percent CI: 6,841–35,526] and 1,000 deaths from ALRI [95 percent CI: 288–1,493] annually among children under age five that would be eliminated if indoor PM_{10} levels were reduced to less than 200 $\mu g/m^3$.

An important question is how this could be achieved. The study by Naeher, Leaderer, and Smith (2000) reports average PM_{10} concentrations and child exposures of less than 200 $\mu g/m^3$ (24-hour average) when well-maintained *planchas* are introduced into houses in which open fires were used previously. Studies that measure indoor concentrations in houses where *planchas* have been used for some time, however, often record higher levels of PM_{10}. This suggests that the benefits (in terms of reduced ALRI in children under age five) of replacing open fires with *planchas* could be less than reported in this study. At the same time, other health benefits (such as benefits to mothers) of reducing IAP in the Guatemalan highlands have not been quantified.

Notes

1. See, for example, Albalak and others 2001; Boy and others 2000; Boy, Bruce, and Delgado 2002; Bruce and others 1998; McCracken and Smith 1998; McCracken and others 1999; Naeher, Leaderer, and Smith 2000; Naeher and others 2000; Naeher and others 2001; and Smith and others 1993.

2. A *plancha mejorada* has an improved combustion chamber.

3. A summary of these studies from Smith and others (2000) is presented in table 3A.1 in the annex to this chapter.

4. According to the 1993 DHS survey (National Council for Population and Development 1993), the under-five mortality rate in the central region of Kenya is 14.7 per 1,000. This rate is comparable to those reported in table 3.5 for Guatemala.

5. In particular, it might lower the odds ratio for the 1,000–2,000 $\mu g/m^3$ category relative to exposure of <500 $\mu g/m^3$.

6. The unexposed incidence rate, m, may be calculated by solving the following equation:

$$\text{Observed incidence rate} = P * OR * m + (1 - P) * m,$$

where P = proportion of children exposed to IAP and OR = odds ratio (here 2.33).

7. The correlation between the case-fatality rate and the percentage of the population in poverty is 0.19 including Quetzaltenango and 0.67 excluding Quetzaltenango. It is possible that case fatality rates do not differ by *departamento* but only appear to do so. This could be the result of greater underreporting of ALRI morbidity in poorer *departamentos*, relative to underreporting of mortality.

Annex 3A. Summary of Epidemiological Studies Relating Indoor Air Pollution to Acute Respiratory Infection

Table 3A.1 Biomass Fuel Use and ALRI in Children under Age Five in Developing Countries

Study	Design	Case Definition	Exposure	Confounding	Comments	OR (95% CI)
Rural South Africa (1980) Natal (Kossove 1982)	Case control, 0–12 months, 132 cases, 18 controls	Outpatients Cases: Wheezing, bronchiolitis, and ALRI; Clinical + x-ray. Controls: Non-respiratory problems	Asked: "Does the child stay in the smoke?" Prevalence = 33%	Routine data collection •number of siblings •economic status Examined, not adjusted	Only 63% of 123 x-rayed had pneumonic changes. Control group was small. Exposure assessment was vague.	4.8 (1.7 to 13.6)
Rural Nepal (1984–85) Kathmandu Valley (Pandey and others 1989)	Cohort, 0–23 months, 780 (study 1) 455 (study 2)	Weekly home visits: ARI grades I–IV (Goroka) breathlessness	Asked mothers for average hours per day the child near fireplace. In Study 1, same team asked about exposure and ARI, therefore bias possible. 77% exposed over 1 hour	Since homes were "homogeneous," confounding not taken into account	Dose-response relationship found. Exposure assessment not validated.	2.2 (1.6 to 3.0)

42

| Rural Gambia (1987–88) Basse (Campbell, Armstrong, and Byass 1989) | Cohort, 0–11 months, 280 | Weekly surveillance. Mother's history of "difficulty with breathing" over subsequent 3-month-period | Reported carriage of child on the mother's back. Prevalence = 37% | Adjusted for •birth interval •parental ETS •crowding •socioeconomic score •nutritional indicators •vaccination status •number of health center visits •ethnic group •maternal education | Father's ETS only other significant factor. Cautious about interpretation, ability to deal with confounding, and to establish causation where exposure and incidence high. | 2.8 (1.3 to 6.1) |
| Urban Argentina (1984–87) Buenos Aires (Cerqueiro and others 1990) | Case control, 0–59 months. Cases: 516 inpatients; 153 outpatients. Controls: 669. | Three hospitals. Cases: ALRI within previous 12 days. Controls: well-baby clinic or vaccination, matched by age, sex, nutritional status, socioeconomic level, date visit, residence. | Interview with mother: Household heating by charcoal; heating with any fuel; bottled gas for cooking | None, but success of matching verified. Multivariate analysis "currently under way" | No data available on charcoal heating in outpatient households. Chimney smoke nearby found to be associated (OR = 2.5–2.7) with ALRI in both kinds of patients. ETS not significant for either. | 9.9 (1.8 to 31.4) for charcoal heat for inpatient, 1.6 (1.3 to 2.0) for any heating fuel in inpatients, 2.2 (1.2 to 3.9) for gas cooking in outpatients. |

(Table continues on the following page.)

Table 3A.1 (*continued*)

Study	Design	Case Definition	Exposure	Confounding	Comments	OR (95% CI)
Rural Zimbabwe Marondera (Collings, Sithole, and Martin 1990)	Case control, 0–35 months, 244 cases, 500 controls	Hospital: Cases: Hospitalized ALRI, clinical and x-ray Controls: Local well-baby clinic	(a) Questionnaire on cooking/ exposure to woodsmoke (b) COHb (all) (c) TSP (2 hr. during cooking): 20 ALRI and 20 AURI cases 73% exposed to open fire	Questionnaire: •maternal ETS •overcrowding •housing conditions •school-age siblings •paternal occupation not adjusted	Confounding: only difference was number of school-age siblings, but not adjusted. COHb not different between ALRI and AURI. TSP means: ALRI (n = 18) 1915 mg/m³ AURI (n = 15) 546 mg/m³.	2.2 (1.4 to 3.3)
Rural Gambia Upper River (Armstrong and Campbell 1991)	Cohort, 0–59 months, 500 (approx)	Weekly home visits: ALRI clinical and x-ray	Questionnaire: Carriage on mother's back while cooking	Questionnaire: •parental ETS •crowding •socioeconomic index •number of siblings •sharing bedroom •vitamin A intake •number of wives •number of clinic visits Adjusted in MLR	Boy/girl difference could be due to greater exposure of young girls. Report carriage on back quite a distinct behavior so should define the two groups fairly clearly with low level of misclassification.	Approach (1) (all episodes) M: 0.5 (0.2 to 1.2) F: 1.9 (1.0 to 3.9) Approach (2) (1st episode) M: 0.5 (0.2 to 1.3) F: 6.0 (1.1 to 34.2)

Urban Nigeria (1985–86) Ibadan: (Johnson and Aderele 1992)	Case control, $n = 103$[cases] + 103 [controls], 0–59 months	Cases: hospitalized ALRI (croup, bronchiolitis, pneumonia, emphysema thoracis) based on clinical, x-ray, and biolab workup. Controls: infant welfare clinic, age and sex matched, no respiratory disease.	Interview: Type of cooking fuel used at home (wood, kerosene, gas)	None	Age, nutritional status, ETS, crowding, and location of cooking area also not significantly associated with ALRI.	NS
Urban Nigeria (1985–86) Ibadan: (Johnson and Aderele 1992)	Case fatality, $n = 103$, 0–59 months	Cases: Death in hospital among ALRI patients (see above)	Interview: Type of cooking fuel used at home (kerosene = 79, gas = 5, wood = 16, other = 3)	None	Overall case fatality rate = 7.8%. 5 of 8 deaths were from wood-burning homes; one additional death had partial exposure to woodsmoke. Poor nutrition (1.8x), low income (1.5x), low maternal literacy (2.1x) were more frequent in wood-burning homes. ETS rates were similar. Yet, paternal income, maternal education, household crowding, ETS not related to case fatality rate.	12.2 ($p < 0.0005$) for those exposed to wood smoke compared to those exposed to kerosene and gas.

(Table continues on the following page.)

Table 3A.1 (*continued*)

Study	Design	Case Definition	Exposure	Confounding	Comments	OR (95% CI)
Rural Tanzania (1986–87) Bagamoyo District (Mtango and others 1992)	Case control Cases: ALRI deaths = 154; Other deaths = 456. Controls = 1,160; 0–59 months	Cases: Verbal autopsy certified by physician of all deaths in period. Controls: Multistage sampling (40 of 76 villages). Children with ALRI were excluded.	Household interview; child sleeps in room where cooking is done; cook with wood	Adjusted for: • village • age • questionnaire respondent • maternal education • parity • water source • child eating habit • whether mother alone decides treatment	About 95% of all groups cook with wood. No tendency to be different distances from road. Perhaps confusion of ALRI with other diseases (for example, measles). Water not from tap had OR = 11.9 (5.5 to 25.7). Models with all deaths—pneumonia deaths, and nonpneumonia deaths had same significant risk factors. No difference in source of treatment by location where child sleeps. Maternal education, religion, crowding, and ETS not significant.	All deaths: 2.8 (1.8 to 4.3) for sleeping in room with cooking. 4.3 for pneumonia only; 2.4 for other deaths.

Study (location, reference)	Design/sample	Cases/Controls	Exposure assessment	Adjustment / comments	Results (OR, 95% CI)
Rural Gambia Upper River (de Francisco and others 1993)	Case control Cases: 129 ALRI deaths. Controls: 144 other deaths. 270 live controls 0–23 months	Cases: Verbal autopsy confirmed by 2 of 3 physicians. Controls: Matched by age, sex, ethnic group, season of death, and geographic area	Indoor air pollution index based on location and type of stove, carrying of child while cooking, and parental ETS (details not provided)	Cases vs. live controls: Adjusted for significant factors in univariate analysis: • socioeconomic score • crowding • parental ETS • nutrition indicators • maternal education. No significant factor for cases vs. dead controls	Only other significant risk factor remaining after multiple conditional logistic regression was whether child ever visited welfare clinic OR = 0.14 (0.06 to 0.36). Misclassification of ALRI deaths (for example, confusion with malaria) is possible reason for lack of significant difference between cases and dead controls. — 5.2 (1.7 to 15.9) for cases vs. live controls.
Urban Brazil (1990) Porto Alegre (Victora and others 1994)	Case control, 0–23 months, 510 cases, 510 controls	Cases: ALRI admitted to hospital; clinical and x-ray. Controls: Age matched, neighborhood	Trained field worker interview: • Any source of indoor smoke (open fires, woodstoves, fireplaces) • usually in kitchen while cooking	Interview: • cigarettes smoked • housing quality • other children in household • income and education • day center attendance • history of respiratory illness • (other) Hierarchical model/MLR	Only 6% of children exposed to indoor smoke. Urban population with relatively good access to health care. Not representative of other settings in developing countries. — Indoor smoke: 1.1 (0.61 to 1.98) Usually in the kitchen: 0.97 (0.75 to 1.26)

(Table continues on the following page.)

Table 3A.1 (*continued*)

Study	Design	Case Definition	Exposure	Confounding	Comments	OR (95% CI)
Urban and Rural India (1991) South Kerala-Trivandrum (Shah and others 1994)	Case control, 2–60 months, 400 total	Hospital. Cases: Admitted for severe to very severe ARI (WHO definition). Controls: Outpatients with nonsevere ARI.	History taken, including •type of stove, with "smokeless" category •outdoor pollution	History: •smokers in house •number of siblings •house characteristics •socioeconomic conditions •education •birth weight and so forth Adjusted in MLR	This is a study of the risk factors for increased severity, as the controls have ARI (nonsevere). On MLR, only age, sharing a bedroom, and immunization were significant. Exposure assessment was vague and unvalidated.	"Smokeless" stove: 0.82 (0.46 to 1.43).
Rural Gambia (1989–1991) Upper River (O'Dempsey and others 1996)	Prospective case control, n = 80 [cases] + 159 [controls], 0–59 months	Attending clinic. Cases: if high respiratory rate, transported to Medical Research Council facility where physician diagnosed pneumonia after lab tests and x-ray. Controls: selected randomly from neighborhood of cases, matched by age.	Household questionnaire: Mother carries child while cooking	Adjusted for: •mother's income •ETS •child's weight slope •recent illness •significant illness in last six months	No effect of bed nets, crowding, wealth, parental education, paternal occupation, age of weaning, and nutritional status. ETS OR = 3.0 (1.1 to 8.1). Etiological (preventive) fraction for eliminating maternal carriage while cooking = 39%; for eliminating ETS in house = 31%. May be reverse causality, that is, sick children being more likely to be carried.	2.5 (1.0 to 6.6)

Source: Smith and others 2000.

OR = Odds Ratio; AURI = Acute Upper Respiratory Infection; COHb = Carboxyhemoglobin; MLR = Maximum Likelihood Ratio; TSP = Total Suspended Particulates; M = Masculine; F = Feminine; ETS = environmental tobacco smoke; NS = not significant.

4

The Evolution of Improved Stoves in Guatemala: Lessons from Three Programs

The modern, efficient biomass stove is an important socioeconomic bridge for people in developing countries who have access to low-cost, readily available biomass but who cannot afford expensive modern fuels. The many potential benefits of such stoves include fuel economy, convenience, and the ability to reduce smoke inside the kitchen. The stoves also offer the environmental benefit of reducing deforestation.

This chapter investigates the potential of an improved stoves program to alleviate the problem of indoor air pollution. It first examines the technical development of wood stoves in Guatemala, and concludes with a review of three of the programs currently promoting the use of these improved stoves.

Development of Improved Stoves in Guatemala

In the 19th century, imports from Europe brought the first significant innovations in wood-burning stoves to Guatemala. In Europe the primary purpose of the stove was to provide indoor heat, but some were also equipped with a metal plate cut with holes, the diameter of which could be modified with rings and moveable covers for cooking. The casting typically was high quality, and some of these stoves are still in use today. In Guatemala, manufacturers reproduced these designs at lower cost and with lower specifications for their own customers. During this period and later, both the imported and home-produced models could be afforded only by the wealthy. The stoves were bought in part to reduce the dirty, irritating smoke that was produced by cooking fires, but typically were supplemented by an open fire outside the kitchen. Some were specially modified to cook food for sale in markets. Metal *planchas* of varying origin and form first began to be used for cooking during this period.

This style of cooking, employing an enclosed, controlled wood fire and controlled emissions, provided the basic format for the commercial wood stoves that followed. The purchaser bought the stove and installed it in the house. A bricklayer or plumber was hired to prepare it for use, and in short

49

order the stove was integrated into the functioning of the home. It was fundamental to these first commercial models that they were produced by an enterprise as a complete metal stove, and then custom-installed in the home. (See table 4.1 for a brief description of all stages of stove development.)

Technological Innovation (1976–1980)

The early versions of the stoves promoted through today's improved stoves program in Guatemala had their foundation at the ICADA Choquí Experimental Station, operating in the western *altiplano* of Guatemala, with a single office in the *departamento* of Quetzaltenango. The station first began its research on alternative technologies for renewable energy applications in the early 1970s. The program has multiple purposes, including the promotion of solar energy to heat water and dry agricultural products, the use of organic fertilizers, soil conservation practices, and the evaluation of wind generation for motive power. The ICADA Choquí Experimental Station's approach to undertaking work in its rural area of operations embraces methodologies similar to those developed in Asia and Africa for promoting alternative energy as a way to alleviate the problems of poverty in remote areas.

During this period the basic philosophy of technology promotion influenced the development and the design of improved stoves. Planners included, for example, the intensive use of local labor and materials in the manufacture of the stoves. The stoves themselves often were self-constructed by local users. These development activities usually required only small financial investments and were based on simple procedures that would support the easy and extensive transfer and application of knowledge and experience. The use of local or traditional technology was also emphasized. Most projects were developed around the use of clay.

A natural disaster in 1976 gave birth to the first prototype of what was to be termed the Lorena stove. Following an earthquake, the Choquí Station decided to consolidate its various small projects into a single program for improved stoves. Technical experts from Canada and the United States were invited to participate in the program. The first prototype of the Lorena stove soon emerged, accompanied by printed informational pamphlets; dissemination of the stove followed.

The Lorena Stove

The Lorena stove was named for the primary materials from which it was manufactured: *lodo* and *arena*, earth and sand. Because the clay and sand were formed into the stove within each individual house, the stove did not come with precise rules for its dimensions. The size and shape would depend on the space and materials available to each user—stoves were made round,

Table 4.1 Stages in the Development of Stove Technology

19th Century	1976–80	1980–1986	1986–1993	1993–2001	2001–Present
Models that predate improved stoves	*Technological innovation*	*Technological diversification*	*Production and dissemination of studies*	*Promotion of commercial models of stoves*	*Beginning of the commercial market period*
• Imported cast-iron stoves • Domestically produced cast-iron stoves • Stoves made from brick, with *planchas* made of cast iron	• The innovative Lorena stove	• Large-scale models based on the Lorena stove • The innovative technology of the Center for Appropriate Technology Research (CETA) stove • Diversification of prefabricated models based on the CETA stove	• National Survey on Improved Stoves • Baseline Study on Tortilla Stoves in Guatemala City • The International Workshop of FWD[a] • Market Study on Stoves in the Guatemala City Metropolitan Area • Study of Indoor Air Pollution from Smoke in Rural Households	• Ubicación del Modelo de Plancha Armada (Location of the *plancha armada* model) • Training programs in *planchas* manufacturing • Development of a prototype *plancha armada* stove • Large-scale distribution of *plancha armada* stoves • Development of commercial models	• Studies conducted on the health impact of the stoves on users • Introduction of portable commercial models based on the *plancha armada* stove • Emphasis on participation by women in stove programs

Source: Fundación Solar 2002.

a. From October 4–10, 1987, a workshop titled "The International Workshop in Dissemination of Woodstoves" was held in Guatemala with support from the International Development Research Centre (IDRC) of Canada and the Foundation for Woodstove Dissemination (FWD), and organized by the Mesoamerican Center for the Study of Appropriate Technology. A main focus of the workshop was to review the Guatemalan program. Portable models of stoves from Africa and Asia were presented.

square, rectangular, and even triangular, to fit into the corner of a room—but the firebox, the diameter of internal passages, the opening through which firewood was added, and the height of the chimney were broadly uniform. No special tools were needed for construction, and measurements were made using hands and fingers. Each stove, as a result, performed differently.

From these modest beginnings, the Lorena stove and its variants spread through local and international donor organizations. The consequence was the large-scale dissemination of the technology. The financing of most projects carried out in this period depended on donations by national and international organizations, which came to be widely known and highly regarded.

In response to the success of the Lorena program, the Guatemala Ministry of Energy and Mines (MEM) formed the National Group for Improved Stoves. Working groups were organized under the Office of Alternative and Renewable Energy to coordinate and promote efforts to disseminate the technology.[1] In 1982 roughly 30 institutions were active in this field, enabling the working groups to be organized to address various special interests, including the recommendations of the Seventh National Congress of Engineering, held that same year, and those of the Third Latin American Conference on Bioenergy. Institutions and individuals that were not involved in these working groups continued to operate independently with their own resources.

At its most fully developed, the National Group for Improved Stoves comprised 27 formally registered institutions from the public and private sector. These institutions exchanged ideas, logistics, information, and technical resources, while trying to keep out of each other's way. The idea behind this organization was to make the most of the resources available for the benefit of all institutions and to assist the work of each member group. The achievements of the energy groups included the formulation of a national program to develop improved stoves, integration of the institutions working in this field, the organization of an interinstitutional information system, and the preparation of a workshop seminar on the construction, use, maintenance, and diffusion of improved stoves. A directory of the national group was put together and a National Survey of Improved Stoves carried out. With the normal progression of change in the administration and of government officials, however, the national group began to decline by 1986.

Studies on and Decline of Improved Stoves (1986–1993)

The isolation of the improved stoves programs that is apparent in Guatemala today had its roots in the late 1980s. The energized period of dissemination of the Lorena stove took a turn for the worse in the mid-1980s. Although there were still a significant number of projects being carried out during

this period, there also was a fairly high turnover in the number of participants: stove promotion groups would disappear and, depending on donor
funding, new ones would emerge. Part of the reason for this change was
the disappearance of the National Group for Improved Stoves.

Although the stove implementation period continued, the tangible
impacts and results were declining. The previously favorable diversification in the program began to show serious deficiencies, and the models that
were successful when new began to have technical problems as they aged.
Consumers started to abandon them. A key part of any program is whether
consumers will purchase a new stove after the old one wears out. In this
case new stoves could no longer be found at the place where the old ones
were built, and people reverted to their old ways of cooking.

Critics of the stove programs consider these outcomes to be a significant
problem, but manufacturers and institutions nonetheless continued their
work, confident in their familiarity with the stoves they had learned to
make. Various documents and research meetings determined, however,
that the only way to coordinate these efforts and to standardize the technology would be to bring all models to formal commercialization.

Promotion of Commercial Models of Improved Stoves (1993–2001)

Partly because of the failure of consumers to purchase new stoves when
their old ones wore out, in the early 1990s it was decided that the stove program should be made subject to the forces of supply and demand. The
theory was that through their market decisions stove users would define
their likes and dislikes of the various features and models of improved
stoves. However, the stoves offered in Guatemala could not be readily trans-
ported once purchased, and the manufacturers could not maintain a reli-
able source of supply to meet large demand, as well as maintain consistent
quality at reasonable prices. The quality of models built almost entirely on
site—the defining feature and abiding problem of the Lorena stove—
furthermore could not be controlled because each model was a different
size and shape.

Meanwhile, the successful use of metal components in the propane stoves
that were made for commercial tortilla producers opened the possibility of
using metal parts to address the problems of quality control and durability
that plagued clay stoves. The idea evolved into the use of a tortilla pan
(*comal*) in the already commercialized cast-iron *planchas*. In the northern
part of Guatemala, it was discovered that people were already using a
plancha armada, a sheet of metal welded to a metal frame, for cooking. Some
models were developed using the *plancha* and trials were conducted by providing them to food vendors in markets or on the street. After the trials,
there was widespread use of the metal *plancha* in the stove models made
during the 1993–2001 period. Institutions and cooperative organizations

Figure 4.1 Typical Plancha Stove Promoted by the Social Fund in Guatemala

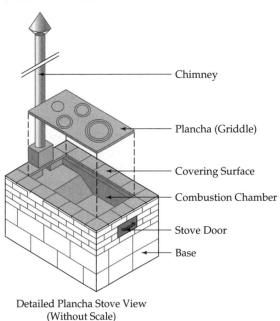

Chimney

Plancha (Griddle)

Covering Surface

Combustion Chamber

Stove Door

Base

Detailed Plancha Stove View
(Without Scale)

Source: Fundación Solar 2002.

fostered the development of new models based on the concept of a *plancha* incorporated into an energy-efficient stove, with a chimney to remove smoke from the house. (See figure 4.1.)

In 1994 and 1995 MEM put together a training program for making *planchas armada* and for building stoves. The program was to run in a place designated the "workshop school," and the training events were to be attended by artisans who wanted to start their own businesses. The underlying principle was that the various procedures in use around the country would be standardized, and a fundamental level of quality control thus maintained for the finished stoves (MEM 2001).

Beginning of Commercial Distribution (2001)

The extensive diffusion of the new stove model led to the development of further new types of programs and projects, notably those financed by government social funds. The process of negotiating and signing the peace agreements that ended the war brought a great deal of international financial assistance to Guatemala, which made this activity a form of household improvement. New programs and projects arose, such as those of the social funds—the Social Investment Fund (FIS), the National Fund for Peace (FONAPAZ), the Fund for Indigenous Development (FODIGUA), and others that carried out work according to their own plans and with little coordination between them. During the mid-1990s, most of the responsibility and financing for improved stoves was moved from MEM to these social funds.

The later part of this period is similar to the first phase in the history of stove development, in that there emerged many new models based on the original design that had been developed to improve stove performance and lower prices. At the Mesoamerican Exchange on Efficient Cooking Techniques and Improved Stoves, organized by Fundación Solar and held in Antigua in August 2001, there were demonstrations of new stove models and techniques for preparing food. The innovations presented had two common principal characteristics—portability, and the use of metal *planchas* in their construction. For example, a new flat *plancha* was on display, constructed in several sections and with different holes so that it could be used in various configurations. The exhibit also included a stove that employed natural convection and was made of fewer parts and required less firewood. Smaller, fixed and portable prefabricated models also were demonstrated that were made of lightweight concrete pieces.

Despite all these innovations, the dominant stove program in rural Guatemala continues to revolve around the stove promoted by the FIS. The FIS is a rural and social development program that offers community grants for making local improvements to schools, water supply, local facilities, and other development projects. As one of the options, the FIS offers community grants for improved stoves. Without much alteration, the original stove design developed by MEM was adopted as the only model of improved stove that would be promoted under the FIS program. As indicated, the program offers communities the possibility of receiving mostly grant funds for programs of their own choosing, and the improved stoves program has been a popular choice for the use of these funds.

Description of Research and Main Issues

To determine the best future direction of the improved stoves program in Guatemala, three relatively successful programs were examined. The programs selected for the case studies were chosen based on a variety of characteristics, including the success of the program, as gauged by its ability to achieve a high and sustained adoption rate of improved stoves; on government and nongovernment involvement; and on geographical diversity. The case studies were carried out in communities selected to reflect broad geographical coverage and for their relatively high rates of stove penetration. They were carried out for the insights they offer into the merits of each program; they are not intended to be program evaluations or market studies. (See table 4.2.)

Table 4.2 Communities Selected for the Study

Organization	Community 1	Stoves in project	Community 2	Stoves in project
Tezulutlán	Quiaté, San Miguel Chicaj, Baja Verapaz	74	Pahoj, Rabinal, Baja Verapaz	28
FIS	Los Achiotes, Jalapa, Jalapa	28	Los González, Jalapa, Jalapa	65
Intervida	San Antonio Las Barrancas, Sibinal, San Marcos	41	Cantel, San Pedro Sacatepéquez, San Marcos	50

Source: Fundación Solar 2002.

Main Issues Examined in Stove Programs

The following key issues were identified for evaluation in the case studies.

Stove pricing. The studies examined the pricing of stoves compared to the costs of producing and marketing them. The benefits or problems of producing relatively inexpensive stoves made of local materials were examined and compared with the use of higher-quality components or parts that may be more expensive. How this was related to the market for the stoves was also examined.

Program financing. The appropriate level of program financing can involve a delicate balance between the size and the delivery mechanism of a subsidy and the pricing of stoves such that they are affordable to poor households. In most internationally successful programs, the stove price does not contain a large subsidy component; governments typically provide financial support (for development costs) and technical assistance to the programs.

Market identification. The use of surveys and other market assessment techniques has been an essential component of most successful programs.

Identification and development of stove types to be promoted in the program. Many internationally successful programs have required an iterative process of development and test marketing under real conditions.

Customer service and satisfaction. The case studies evaluated both the impact of stoves on rural communities and the degree of consumer satisfaction with the stoves, focusing on the techniques used to sell and service the stoves.

Operational procedure. Operational procedures included the allocation of institutional responsibilities, the allocation of work, and training at the community level or for artisans.

Communication and promotion. Communication and promotion of stoves is often a key component in a successful program, especially for the executing agency, the stove manufacturers, and the rural beneficiaries.

Local perception. Consideration of the needs and views of consumers has been a hallmark of most successful programs. Do consumers value the stoves because they save energy, are convenient, or eliminate indoor air pollution? What types of modification would the consumer like to see made to the stove?

Design of the Study

The three projects were chosen as case studies based on their locations, differences in the availability of firewood (some had abundant supplies and others scarce supplies), beneficiaries from various indigenous ethnic groups as well as the Ladinos, and the use of different project implementation methodologies, including different levels of subsidy. Together, the three projects are fairly representative of the projects carried out in other parts of Guatemala. The programs include the FIS project, which is national in scope; the Intervida project, located in various *departamentos* in western Guatemala; and the Tezulutlán project, which covers a number of municipalities in the northern *departamento* of Baja Verapaz (table 4.2). Once the projects were selected, a preliminary list of communities was compiled, and for each project two communities were then chosen that best met the selection criteria.

Conducting the case studies involved collecting information from a variety of different sources. Several sources were used to gather secondary information on population, economic status, housing, means of access and transport, and poverty maps in the study areas. First, field teams were formed to gather the data. Facilitators were needed to conduct the interviews with stove users, especially in the case of the study carried out in the *departamento* of San Marcos, an area with a predominantly indigenous population. Second, the regional offices of the various projects were visited to interview technicians and extension workers and to learn about their work methodologies. Third, selected communities and community leaders were contacted to ask for their help in gathering information and organizing focus group interviews. (Leaders in all the selected communities offered their support, which greatly eased the process of information gathering.) Finally, the team interviewed the owners and employees of the metalworking shops that sell components and that manufacture the improved stoves.

Background on Stoves Program Case Studies

The three stove programs examined in this chapter include one financed by the European Union (EU), another funded by the government of Spain, and a third supported and implemented by the Guatemala Social Investment Fund (Fondo de Inversíon Social; FIS). This section provides brief background for the programs and their methods of implementation.

The Tezulutlán Project: Integrating Stoves with Rural Development

The Tezulutlán project was an integrated rural development project that started in 1999 and is still in operation in 2005. The funding for the project was provided jointly by the government of Guatemala (covering personnel expenses) and the EU (most of the physical investments). The project focused mainly on agricultural extension, as well as health and nutrition; the stoves component was implemented under the health and nutrition component and initiated in 1999. It continued for about three years. From the beginning, the principal goal of the stove component was to improve living conditions for rural populations, paying special attention to women, hygiene, health, and household improvement. In pursuit of this goal, the project looked specifically to build an improved, wood-conserving stove that would improve the indoor environment of users.

The Tezulutlán project was implemented in the *departamento* of Baja Verapaz in the northern region, north of Guatemala City. The *departamento* is 3,124 square kilometers in size, with a low population density of 68 people per square kilometer (compared to the national average of 103 people per square kilometer). The proportion of the population living in rural areas is relatively high, at 78 percent. The literacy rate, at 56 percent, is low. The *departamento's* poverty rate is 72 percent, with 31 percent living in extreme poverty. The economy of the region is based on agriculture, primarily sugar cane, vegetables, basic grains, and cereals. The climate in most of the *departamento* is dry. Many communities suffer from significant deforestation and a shortage of firewood (INE 1994).

There were several phases to the implementation of the Tezulutlán project, beginning with analysis of existing stove models in the various municipalities of Salamá and continuing ultimately to visits by monitors to verify the quality and proper use of the installed stoves. Tezulutlán conducted the first research on the improved stoves, discovering that some models still used too much firewood. The project evaluated the various types of stoves that were in common use,[2] with the goal of developing a stove that would combine the best features of the stoves being promoted and installed by the diverse development organizations operating in the *departamento* of Baja Verapaz (Baja Verapaz 2002). In this it enlisted the insight and advice of the local women who were using the stoves.

Once the new stove had been designed (see figure 4.2), the work of promoting it began. With the help of field staff, the project delivered 4,129 improved, wood-conserving stoves during the three years of implementation. The project sought the participation of other NGOs that operated in the area, providing them with financial support and technical assistance for installing the stoves. The project provided the funds necessary to contract with the extension workers, who remained part of their NGO

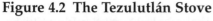

Figure 4.2 The Tezulutlán Stove

Photo from Tezulutlán project. Note the clay chimney, lack of a stove door, and the shelf for holding up the fuelwood so that it can be fed into the stove once the wood inside is burned up.

Source: Fundación Solar.

teams—Tezulutlán became a source of technical and financial support for the NGOs that were already operating in the area, so that they could foster the use of the improved stoves and make the intervention sustainable.

The Intervida Program: Focus on Children, Families, and Poverty

Intervida is a Spanish NGO that supports community development in Guatemala and in six other countries through sponsored-child programs. The goal of the program in Guatemala is to improve the lives of women and children through training and community organization, cultural events, education, community infrastructure, income-generating initiatives, health, and food security. Established in Guatemala in 1996, Intervida focuses its activities on the western highlands.

There are three main components to Intervida's work in Guatemala. The Community Support, Organization, and Training program provides the foundation for other programs, strengthening community organization and forming community committees to manage the projects. The Basic Support program focuses on health and education, and is responsible primarily for medical visits and school construction. Finally, the Production and Marketing program seeks to stimulate the economy and to generate income through its work in livestock, agriculture, forestry, and community organization.

The Intervida project to promote wood-saving stoves began in 1998, in response to public demand. The project was undertaken by the Production and Marketing Program, because Intervida sought to encourage communities to make a strong commitment to the project (and to share some of the cost of the stoves). The Basic Support program also initiated a program of installing improved stoves in schools. From 1998 to 2000 the household project grew steadily: In the *departamento* of San Marcos, 142 stoves were installed in 1998, 1,200 in 1999, and 2,000 in 2000. In 2001 the number of stoves installed fell to about 500. The Production and Marketing component generally is flexible in terms of its work strategy, with its principal objective being the promotion of economic development in the communities in which it works. To achieve this objective, Intervida designs work plans and strategies that seek out feedback and that aim to be constantly adaptable, as was demonstrated by the stoves program. The objectives of the wood-saving stoves program were the following: to save firewood, to benefit both the environment and family budgets; to improve the home by reducing indoor air pollution; and to use and manage natural resources sustainably.

As of the end of 2000, projects implemented in the western part of the country had installed 8,500 stoves, though after that year stove production at the household level declined significantly, with only about 500 stoves installed in 2001. One of the main lessons learned was that projects for wood-saving stoves require strong community participation. One example of a typical *plancha* Intervida stove in Quetzaltenango region is depicted in figure 4.3. Note that the stove door is open and the chimney has been replaced by a cement pipe.

Figure 4.3 An Example of an Intervida-Type Stove

Source: Intervida.

The stove project has since been refocused on an integrated watershed management project that will last 10 years, from 2001 to 2010. Within this watershed project the communities involved are to carry out wood-saving stove projects as well as integrated projects in the fields of forestry, agriculture, and livestock. The stove project is implemented under the condition that each beneficiary pays back the cost of the stove (approximately US$100) over a one-year period; these funds are subsequently used as seed money for investment in other projects in the forestry, agriculture, and livestock areas.

The FIS Program: Successful Government Program with Limited Flexibility

The FIS is a decentralized, government entity with administrative autonomy and with its own legal standing and heritage. The FIS was created in the aftermath of the war during the late 1990s in Guatemala to provide grants to and make investments in activities that improve the quality of life for the rural poor. The main working groups within the FIS are focused on the environment; productive projects; water and sanitation; and education, health, and nutrition. The three fundamental goals of its work are to provide technical assistance, to finance development projects, and to strengthen community self-management. The FIS has nationwide coverage through 24 departmental offices.

The stoves program is the responsibility of the FIS Environment Unit—and due to the demand for improved stoves from rural communities, is the unit's largest responsibility. Inaugurated in 1996, the program is based primarily on promotion of *plancha*-type stoves developed from a FIS prototype that was designed originally for members of impoverished groups or communities in rural areas, to replace worn-out stoves or as an alternative to the open fire. The main changes to the prototype since the beginning of the project have centered on the metal *plancha*, or hot plate.

The FIS stoves program has proven exceedingly popular. FIS stoves have been installed throughout the country, and the technology is familiar to many rural communities. The demand for stove projects continues to be robust, and it is estimated that approximately 15,000 stoves are built each year. By the end of 2001, an estimated 90,000 stoves had been built in rural homes in Guatemala and most of them were completed under the FIS program.

The main FIS stove has a metal *plancha* with four holes for cooking (see figure 4.4). This model has been used since the beginning of the program, with the only significant change being replacement of the 8 mm cast-iron *plancha* by one made of 5mm *armado* iron.[3] It is generally accepted that the newer *plancha* is both of better quality and is cheaper than the older cast-iron version. No technical data support this perception, but because the FIS

Figure 4.4 Stoves in Rural Households

Source: Photos by Fundación Solar and Rogério Carneiro de Miranda.
Note: Typical *plancha* stove and FIS stove built in 2001.

program, the Tezulutlán project, and Intervida all have independently changed from cast iron to *armado* iron, the anecdotal evidence is strong. The lack of interaction between the three groups that strengthens this perception is, however, a significant weakness in the stoves programs in Guatemala.

Under the FIS program, community groups are organized and given the responsibility to select the development option they favor. The process works as follows: A facilitator calls a meeting of community leaders (religious, legal, and traditional), who together create an association comprising representatives of all sectors of the community. The association members are trained in the method of operation of the FIS, and subsequently convene a community forum to prioritize the short-, medium-, and long-term needs of the community. The FIS provides financing for the highest-priority project on the community's list, provided that the association can manage the project. The principle underlying this process is that the community, through the associations that are formed, will retain the ability to manage other projects in the future, perhaps with other development organizations. In the case of the stoves program, projects that are identified for implementation by the committee are financed by the FIS subject to the availability of funds and to the fulfillment of the conditions for a viable project.

After a technical committee (comprising directors appointed by the FIS executive board) approves a project, private companies contracted through public bidding make the FIS stoves. The contract for the stove construction company is a comprehensive arrangement. The builder is responsible for constructing the complete stove, including the purchase of materials, paying the cost of getting the materials to the community, and paying for skilled labor. The company has to give a one-year guarantee on its work. The construction company is paid as progress in building the stoves is made. Forty percent is paid as an advance at the beginning of the job, followed by three equal payments of approximately 17 percent, the first for building the base, the second for the firebox, and the third for installing the *planchas*, chimneys, and accessories. The remaining 10 percent is paid when the completed stove is handed over.

Comparative Assessment of the Case Studies

The improved stoves program in Guatemala is relatively advanced, compared to programs in other regions in Latin America. There are both good and poor aspects to the program, but it is obvious that it has and continues to receive significant support from both local people and donors. The next section compares the three case studies.

Subsidies and Commercialization of the Stoves Programs

Guatemala's stoves program is unique in that it involves the distribution of fairly substantial and expensive stoves. The stoves are prohibitively expensive for many people, even the least expensive costing more than US$50. Elsewhere in the developing world the stoves promoted by comparable programs typically cost US$5 to US$10. The establishment of a purely commercial market for such an expensive stove in rural areas is out of the question. In spite of this (and due in part to government and donor assistance), rural people place a high priority on getting these stoves.

Because the financing for the stoves does not come from the consumer, the development of a dynamic market for improved stoves has been relatively limited. The stoves programs typically have consisted of isolated activities by projects operating independently. Although most projects are fairly well designed and rural people generally seem to be satisfied with them, such independence and isolation inevitably generate problems. For example, the tendency of each program to produce and sell stoves for about 20 percent of their actual cost (see table 4.3) has created a situation in which the different types of stoves do not compete with each other. This results in market distortions and has given rise to technical deficiencies in some stoves, to the point where it is common for a household to revert to use of an open fire rather than to the "improved" stove. (This is a problem particularly for the FIS and the Intervida programs; the stove developed for the Tezulutlán program appears to be much better used.)

Because each program has its own approved model, there is no competition between the different models. Although most successful programs throughout the world cap the actual subsidies for stoves themselves, in Guatemala the preference for more expensive stoves may limit such an

Table 4.3 Typical Subsidies of Three Programs in Rural Guatemala, 2002

Community	Total number of stoves	Firewood procurement	Percentage using open fire	Improved stove cost to user	Approximate total stove costs (including user cost)
Tezulutlán					
Quiate	74	Gather	12	Q 100 plus materials	Q 500
Pahoj	28	Gather	0	Q 100 plus materials	Q 500
FIS					
Los Achiotes	28	Buy	40	Q 65.5, including materials	Q 800–1,000
Los González	65	Buy and gather	38	Q 65.5, including materials	Q 800–1,000
Intervida					
San Antonio	41	Gather	42	Q 151, including materials	Q 684
Cantel	50	Buy	28	Q 151, including materials	Q 684

Source: Fundación Solar 2002.

Note: Q = Guatemalan quetzales. Eight quetzales are approximately equal to US$ 1.

approach. However, the development of different types of stoves and competition for customers are limited in the programs, and there could be new mechanisms to share experience between the programs. The problems faced by all programs are fairly similar, so it would be beneficial to learn from each program or project's mistakes or successes. The Guatemala FIS program relies heavily on subsidies so there has been no development of a stove market. The only stove model approved by the government receives the subsidy. A government unit or private agency mandated by the government involved with improved stove design could approve a large number of stoves and also have a technical support unit to share experience between programs.

Stove Design Issues and After-Sales Maintenance

The three projects studied all used the same process of trial and error in developing the metal *plancha*, an inevitable duplication of effort given the lack of communication between the programs. All three programs initially used an 8 mm cast-iron *plancha* before arriving independently at the conclusion that a 5 mm *armada plancha* was a better substitute.

The original cast-iron *planchas* suffered from cracking and warping. Of the 15 women in the sample that had trouble with the *plancha*, only three made some type of homemade modification to resolve the problem. This suggests that there is no easy way to repair a *plancha*, and if a *plancha* cracks or warps the likely result is that the house will become smoky again. The *plancha* must, therefore, be of good quality and the stove user must know the limitations on its use and how to properly care for it.

According to the three case studies, the chimney, firebox, and accessories (the door for feeding firewood and the regulator to control airflow) were the source of most of the difficulties that users experienced in operating the stove. In two of the four communities that used chimneys made of zinc sheet metal, some people replaced their 100 mm diameter chimney with one that had a larger diameter. Women in the focus groups also said they prefer a larger chimney because it requires less cleaning. The main problem with the clay chimneys is that they are fragile and therefore difficult to transport. In Baja Verapaz there is only one artisan who produces clay chimneys, so it is hard for people to get a replacement. New chimney parts must be brought in from outside the immediate region, which again is difficult because so many communities are remote and accessible only by poor roads.

Some people in Los González were found to have enlarged the inside of the firebox, because the small volume of the original firebox required them to split their firewood into smaller pieces—an unwelcome extra chore for the families. In San Antonio las Barrancas some users had broken the fireboxes or dislodged the bricks that frame the opening. In Quiaté and Pahoj, where the stoves were built by people from the community, the builders tended from the beginning to make a larger firebox than specified in the design, and also to build a larger opening for feeding the firewood. The design of the firebox used in the Tezulutlán project is different from that of the FIS and Intervida model (see figure 4.5), making it easier to put in larger pieces of wood. The stove builders in the Tezulutlán project also did not put doors on the fireboxes, regarding them as an unnecessary complication.[4]

The community that had the most problems with the firebox was San Antonio las Barrancas. In this community, where the project was implemented in 1998, local men trained by bricklayers built the stoves. It is likely

Figure 4.5 Firebox Differences Between Stoves

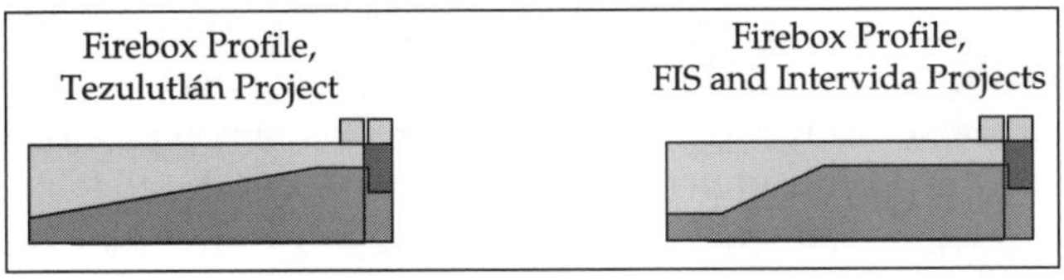

Source: Fundación Solar 2002.

that the problems experienced by users were due to a lack of quality control during construction. The main problem with the firebox was breakage at the point where the bricks meet, which in extreme cases led to a brick coming loose entirely, leaving a gap in the firebox. The chimney, *plancha*, and firebox are critical for the proper functioning of the stove. The incidence of problems for each component in the sample of 87 improved stoves is 18 percent for the chimney, 18 percent for the firebox, 17 percent for the *plancha*, and 16 percent for the accessories (see table 4.4).

The age of the stoves studied ranged from one to four years, and there was a relationship between the age of the stove and the number of problems reported (see table 4.5), mainly in the chimneys and *poyetóns* (bases). The communities studied in the FIS and Intervida projects received no assistance from the projects in making modifications to the stoves or in replacing parts that failed. The communities aided in the Tezulutlán project in contrast received support from the project's technical staff or extension workers during the execution and monitoring phase (the first year using the stove). This program, which placed more emphasis than the other two on stove design, inviting the input of users, appears to have been the most successful in avoiding problems during actual use.

Clearly the process of stove design can have a significant impact on the acceptance of the stove by users and whether they use it as their main cooking device. The experimentation in the Tezulutlán project, including designing a stove without a door, proved to be important for continuing use of the stove. At the very least, there needs to be greater communication among the different programs about the practice of stove design.

User Perceptions of Improved Stoves

The general impression of participants in all three programs is that the improved stoves have had a significant impact on their lives. Participants reported the most valued benefits to be the use of less fuelwood, a reduction in cooking time, and the removal of smoke from the house interior (table 4.6). Given the drudgery involved in collecting firewood and cooking, these are significant benefits for rural women. In Cantel and San Antonio, the reason given for the reduced time spent cooking was that with the multiple stove pot openings the cook can prepare several dishes simultaneously. The respondents also state that the kitchen is cleaner than it was before. While users favorably report removal of smoke from the house, they are unlikely to fully understand the long-term health consequences of this benefit. The advantages of reduced eye irritation and better respiratory health, for example, were perceived to be the lowest benefits under the program. A more highly valued benefit cited by female users is that they no longer have to buy clay *comals*, as they can cook tortillas on the *plancha* of the stove.

Table 4.4 Comparisons of Stove Issues for Six Villages in Three Improved Stove Projects

Community	Project	Year stove was built	Total number of stoves	Sample size	Problems					Replacements or modifications[a]					Changes suggested by users				
					Chimney	Plancha	Firebox	Accessories	Poyetón	Chimney	Plancha	Firebox	Accessories	Poyetón	Change chimney	Size or height of stove	Appearance of stove	Added features[b]	Change poyetón
San Antonio	Intervida	1998	41	14	5	4	5	1	5	7	1			6	•	•		•	•
Los Achiotes	FIS	1999	28	10	5	1	1		4	1	1	1			•				
Quiaté	Tezulutlán	2000	74	17	4	7				4		1		1			•		
Cantel	Intervida	2000	50	18	1	2	9		4										
Pahoj	Tezulutlán	2001	28	7	1	1	1		1	1	1	1		1			•		
Los González	FIS	2001	65	21	1	1	1	7	2	1	1	6		1		•	•	•	
TOTAL			**286**	**87**	**16**	**15**	**16**	**8**	**16**	**13**	**3**	**9**		**9**					

Source: Fundación Solar 2002.

Note: Of all the stoves sampled, only one, in Los Achiotes, was not working.

a. The replacements or modifications made were not always due to failed components.

b. The additional features suggested by users were an oven, a space to store firewood, a clay *comal*, and a water heater.

Table 4.5 Problems with Improved Stove Chimneys in Guatemala, 2002

Community	Chimney construction	Year chimney built	Total number of stoves	Sample size	Number of chimneys with problems	Percentage of chimneys with problems
Tezulutlán						
Quiaté	Clay	2000	74	17	4	24
Pahoj	Clay	2001	28	7	0	0
FIS						
Los Achiotes	Zinc sheet metal	1999	28	10	5	50
Los González	Zinc sheet metal	2001	65	21	1	5
Intervida						
San Antonio	Zinc sheet metal	1998	41	14	5	36
Cantel	Zinc sheet metal	2000	50	18	1	6

Source: Fundación Solar 2002.

Some suggestions for improvements were also offered. In San Antonio, almost 60 percent of those interviewed complained that the stove does not heat the house. Other suggestions were to enlarge the chimney and to add space to the stove for storing firewood.[5] It was also suggested that the chimney might be made out of cement or bricks instead of sheet metal, that the stove could include an oven and water heater, and that the platform could be made out of cinder blocks or brick instead of adobe. In San Antonio, female users said they would prefer the stove to be lower and the opening for firewood larger. In almost total contrast, interviews with users in Cantel came up with only one objector, who suggested that the stove was too low. No other users in Cantel raised any objections at all.

The women in Los Achiotes made several observations about the disadvantages of the improved stoves. They did not like the limited weight that the *plancha* could support,[6] they felt that there were problems controlling the intensity of the fire, and they suggested that the diameter of the chimney was too small. The criticisms cited by the women in Los González included the major observation that the smoke does not vent out of the house. This complaint was made by 14 percent of users, but it was suggested by program coordinators that the problem might be due to inadequate cleaning of the chimney. A small number of people also indicated it was difficult

Table 4.6 The Benefits of Improved Stoves in Two Programs in Guatemala, 2002

| | Tezulutlán | | | | | | FIS | | | | | |
| | Quiaté | | Pahoj | | Total | | Los Achiotes | | Los González | | Total | |
Benefits	N	%	N	%	N	%	N	%	N	%	N	%
Uses less firewood	14	82	4	57	18	75	8	80	18	86	26	84
Less smoke in the house	12	71	3	43	15	63	7	70	15	71	22	71
Requires less time to cook	11	65	2	29	13	54	6	60	19	90	25	81
Saves time collecting firewood	6	35	2	29	8	33	4	40	8	38	12	39
Kitchen is cleaner	5	29	0	0	5	21	3	30	6	29	9	29
Effect on eyes and respiratory health	4	24	0	0	4	17	4	40	6	29	10	32
Number interviewed	17	100	7	100	24	100	10	100	21	100	31	100

Source: Fundación Solar 2002.

to cook tortillas on the *plancha*, possibly due to problems in controlling the intensity of the fire. In the sample group, however, 52 percent found no disadvantages to using the improved stoves.

Among those people who did not participate in the stoves program, there were a variety of practical reasons for not adopting the stoves. In San Antonio the main reason was that the respondent did not, at the time the project was implemented, have his or her own house (one of the requirements of the program is that the stove be built inside a home). In Cantel, eight people without stoves were interviewed and the main reason they did not get one was lack of money. The people without stoves still use open fires. All of those questioned expressed an interest in getting a stove now that they have seen the advantages of having one. According to these respondents, the advantages of the improved stoves include firewood savings, better cooking performance, the removal of smoke from the house, and the general improvement that the addition of a stove represents to the home. While the main reason cited for not having a stove is cost, all of the women interviewed buy their firewood; it is possible that the savings on firewood that are brought by stove ownership would rapidly offset the cost of the stove itself.

These results indicate that people have definite opinions on how to improve the usability of these stoves. This leads to the topic of the next section: how to improve the design of the stoves through bringing together the key people involved.

Interaction Between Stove Users, Builders, and Designers

One of the most interesting aspects of the case studies relates to the different ways in which the programs seek and use interaction between the users, builders, and designers. Under the FIS program, the stove design basically has been unchanged for the last 10 years. While the stove design originally was the result of collaboration, it has failed to evolve to meet changing needs of users. The Intervida program also sought to create intensive interaction in its early stages, but only the Tezulutlán program maintained significant consultation with local people throughout the installation of the stoves and beyond.

One of the greatest strengths of the Tezulutlán project is the participation of users in the design of the stove. This has helped ensure that the stove is appropriate to the needs and preferences of women in the region. The design itself enables flexibility in construction, as it includes local materials (also bringing down the cost). For example, making the stove out of adobe allows the height of the stove to be adjusted to suit each user. The Tezulutlán stove also has the virtue of having a clay chimney, the outside of which does not become excessively hot, therefore guarding against burns, especially when making tortillas. This is important to the user because tortillas typically are cooked several times each day.

A good indicator of the success of the Tezulutlán project is the fact that stoves built more than three years ago are still working well. In some cases parts have been replaced, but as this has been part of each family's responsibility it helps foster a greater sense of ownership and familiarity with the stove, and thereby reduces the family's dependence on the project's technical staff.

Most of the differences in the Tezulutlán stoves, compared to those of the other programs, were the result of the interactive process between the designers, builders, and users of the stove. The stove retains the basic elements of the common metal *plancha* stove disseminated around the country by the FIS project. These include the stove base, firebox, metal *plancha*, and chimney. The design of the Tezulutlán firebox is different from that of the FIS model (see figure 4.5), however, while the concept of using a small internal volume has been retained. The opening for firewood is a larger 20×20 centimeters, for ease of fueling, but a ramp progressively reduces the internal dimensions so that the back of the chamber is only 10 centimeters high. This small internal volume ensures the efficient use of the heat generated by the fire, which is transmitted directly to the metal *plancha*. This model uses a clay chimney produced by local artisans.

The Tezulutlán model also incorporates a support for the wood to prevent it from falling from the fire. The technical team determined from users that a door to the firebox was superfluous, as few people closed it and many actually took it off. They determined also that the airflow regulator was too difficult to use. As a consequence, both features were omitted from the final design. (The absence of a door or its lack of use is a common feature in the other programs; see figure 4.4.) This simplification of the design has the additional benefit of easing the transfer of the technology. The Tezulutlán *plancha* similarly was modified on the recommendation of users. The first *planchas* were made of cast iron, which sometimes cracked; the design team therefore developed a *plancha* made of reinforced sheets of iron that were available only from a supplier in Guatemala City. Additionally, the new *plancha* had three holes that, based on consultation, were each fitted with removable rings that allow their diameter to be modified to accommodate different sizes of pots.

The FIS and Intervida projects were far less proactive in stove design. The FIS stove has a base of a fixed height, a feature that despite being criticized remains unchanged. While there was apparently some awareness within the task group that carried out the stove projects that the FIS program must focus on the women who use the stoves, there was no evidence that action was being taken to increase the participation of these women in community development or decision making, nor was there any attempt to grant them greater access to resources. Where the Tezulutlán project teams made a positive decision not to have a door for the stove, the FIS project went ahead with doors: In Los González, 35 percent of these doors fell off the firebox and are no longer used. The Intervida project similarly made no effort to invite input from users, nor did it act to promote the participation of women in community decision making or to give them greater access to resources.

For two of the projects, once the stove was designed there was little use of feedback from users to improve that initial design. The Tezulutlán project, in contrast, was able to develop some valuable innovations through collaboration with users and builders. All three programs falter in their failure to communicate with each other, to take advantage of such innovations, and to develop the cross-fertilization of ideas.

Best Features and Problems of Improved Stoves Programs

The improved stoves projects in Guatemala include good practices that should be drawn upon and taken into account in the implementation of a national improved stoves program. They also include weaknesses that should be avoided or addressed. The best features of the programs and the weaknesses of the projects are presented in this section. Both positive and negative aspects of the programs came from the evaluations and the focus discussion groups (table 4.4).

Best Features from the Three Case Studies

The main features of the projects that generally are accepted as positive include the use of methodologies that promote community participation and local capacity building with a focus on women; participation of actual users in the design of the stoves; and commitment by people from the community to help build the stoves (table 4.7).

Because of the multiethnic, multicultural, and multilingual nature of Guatemala, the tendency of the projects to focus on defined geographic areas allowed intensive work to be done with groups of people of similar ethnic and cultural backgrounds. The employment of staff from the project area also facilitated the use of local resources for the projects, improved communications between the project and the communities, and strengthened support and training activities.

The use of stove models that incorporated ergonomic and safety considerations, that were functional, and that provided economic and health benefits also contributed to the uptake of the new technology.

Requiring users to pay part of the stove's cost (the share paid by users was about 40 percent in the Tezulutlán project, 30 percent in Intervida, and 10 percent in the FIS program) helped reduce their dependence on social assistance projects.

Table 4.7 Positive Aspects of the Improved Stoves Project Case Studies

Aspect	Project		
	Tezulutlán	*FIS*	*Intervida*
Institutional	Family focus Participation of women and the family in design and construction of the stove Collective responsibility for the stove Gender focus Reducing dependency on the NGO (contributing 45 percent toward the cost of the stove) Local capacity to support the sustainability of the project Participation by local population	Implementation capacity Job creation (private Guatemalan firms) National scope (Departmental offices) Participation of local population Identifying community priorities through participatory practices Evolution toward greater community participation	Participation of local population Decentralized implementation units Joint NGO–community effort (contributing 30 percent of the stove's value)
Technical	Use of materials available locally Ergonomic criteria used in design Safety criteria used in design Wood-saving design	Wood-saving design Durable materials Replicable	Wood-saving design Durable materials
Financing	Participation of users in paying for the stove (45 percent)	Participation of users in covering part of the stove's cost (10 percent)	Participation of users in covering part of the stove's cost (30 percent)
Commercialization	Marketing of the stove in local hardware stores Support to local artisans		

Source: Fundación Solar 2002.

Weaknesses Found in the Case Studies

There were also some weaknesses in the projects (table 4.8). One glaring weakness was the lack of systematic community feedback, monitoring, and evaluation. The absence of research and technological development, as well as the poor quality of some of the stoves, were obstacles to improvement of the stove models, and they constrained the development of more and better options.

The high subsidies provided for the stoves, as well as the lack of a direct relationship between vendors and users, distorted the market, elevated prices, and constrained development of the commercial structures necessary for the projects to be sustainable.

There was a lack of technical assistance to support modification of the stove models and the sort of innovation that could reduce costs and deliver more effective and efficient models. This situation could be addressed through the use of trials, quality certification, consultations with stove users, and the training of stove builders.

These observations concerning the strengths and the weaknesses of the existing programs provide a context for developing lessons to improve the effectiveness of future work in the area of improved stoves.

Recommendations and Lessons

One-third of rural families use wood exclusively as cooking fuel. Only about 5 percent do not use wood at all. More than 90 percent of rural families still cook over an open fire, with its concomitant dangers of indoor air pollution and accidental burns. The three case studies reviewed in this chapter reveal that people in the communities with improved stoves programs have identified a number of benefits from using these stoves, particularly their ability to save money and to improve conditions in the home, which in turn implies better health conditions. A more structured and coordinated effort for improved stoves would help foster and strengthen the practices used by the existing projects, and thereby would increase the access of people in rural Guatemala to a variety of better-quality, safer stoves.

The lack of coordination among the dynamic stoves programs in Guatemala is a significant problem. The government could play an important role, both in facilitating dialogue among the various parties interested in promoting improved stoves and in ensuring that the public has access to stoves that are durable and of good quality. This section examines strategies to raise the effectiveness of the overall effort to expand the use of better stoves, by improving the effectiveness of existing programs and by linking these with broader rural development programs.

Table 4.8 Weaknesses of the Improved Stoves Project Case Studies

Aspect	Project		
	Tezulutlán	*FIS*	*Intervida*
Institutional	Lack of monitoring during construction Lack of project evaluation Project not self-sustaining	Lack of integration of the project team Centralization of decision making power Lack of feedback No research or technological development work No participation by users in designing the stove No gender focus Not a self-sustaining project	No research or technological development work No participation by users in designing the stove No gender focus Lack of project evaluation Project is not self-sustaining
Technical	Users have little access to some stove components Difficulty transporting the clay chimneys (fragile) Lack of standardization in stove components, affecting efficiency	Poor construction quality	Poor construction quality
Financing	Dependence on international donations Subsidy of some components of the stove: *plancha*, chimney, bricks, and transportation (55 percent)	Dependence on international aid Subsidy for everything except local materials and unskilled labor (90 percent)	Dependence on international aid from the sponsors Subsidy for bricks, *plancha*, chimney, and transportation (70 percent)
Commercialization	No structures created for commercializing the stove (only certain parts of the stove are sold in the municipal seats)	Commercialization only at the project–builder level (dependence on the programs) No structures created for commercializing the stove (only certain parts of the stove are sold in municipal seats)	Commercialization only at the project–builder level (dependence on the programs) No structures created for commercializing the stove (only certain parts of the stove are sold in municipal seats)

Source: Fundación Solar 2002.

Role of Subsidies

The stoves being promoted by the government and various donor agencies in Guatemala involve about an 80 percent subsidy for the purchase of the stove. A high percentage of the remaining 20 percent of the cost that the consumer must bear is accounted for by materials and labor. This situation is a consequence, in part, of the high cost of the type of stove being promoted in Guatemala. At present, the subsidies are tied to specific stove models—mainly those models offered by the program or donor providing the subsidy.

Given that subsidies are an integral part of the improved stoves program in Guatemala, the removal of subsidies would harm the existing programs and would have adverse consequences for the health of rural people. This conclusion is inescapable given the high cost of most of the stoves that are eligible for subsidy, which puts them out of the reach of most rural people.

The recommendation of this chapter is to create a more open process for subsidizing improved stoves. For example, the subsidies provided by FIS could be applied to programs sponsored by nongovernmental organizations (NGOs) or programs affiliated with other donors. Before they could be included in the FIS subsidy program, the models being promoted by the NGOs or donors would have to be tested and certified for reduced energy consumption and for their ability to remove household smoke. Donor investments could then be used for developing new and different kinds of stoves to serve a more diverse rural population. In some areas, for example, it is important to families that the stove produces room heat, as well as improve cooking. If the groups that promote stoves could use the subsidy from the FIS program, they could concentrate their efforts on stove development, project supervision, and the other tasks necessary for a successful program. This process could be further facilitated by the development of a technical assistance unit.

Role of the Market

In Guatemala there is a need for a market structure that would permit a more direct relationship between stove users and the private firms that manufacture stoves. The goal is for retailers selling the stoves to view the user rather than the donor or government as their customer, which in turn would require both the retailer and the manufacturer to develop high-quality stoves and provide a high level of service. Furthermore, a commercial market would, through market demand, give users a voice. However, in the short term, the cost of stoves would seem to make the creation of a market without some kind of subsidy impossible. It additionally should be noted that stove manufacturers are often small businesses with little or no ability to conduct market research into end users' needs and desires.

Studies are therefore necessary to clarify whether subsidies are required for the promotion of improved stoves. Studies would also be important in defining strategies for the retail distribution and marketing of stoves. Any such study would require technical assistance.

Greater Interaction Between Programs: Stove Users, Designers, and Manufacturers

The benefits of greater interaction between stove users, designers, and manufacturers is evident from the case study of the Tezulutlán project, and the experience of such programs could be invaluable for other groups entering the business of promoting improved stoves. One of the major problems in the overall stoves program in Guatemala today, however, is that the lack of cooperation and communication between programs means that, in a sense, each new program must reinvent the stove.

We therefore recommend that technical assistance be provided to an NGO or national agency to assist it in prompting interaction between the parties involved in the design and marketing of improved stoves. The lessons learned by the various programs need to be shared among all groups involved in the promotion of improved stoves, to eliminate duplication of effort and to help deliver the best stoves programs possible.

Institutional Roles and Participants for Promoting Improved Stoves

To implement these recommendations to improve the effectiveness of current programs, we recommend that the government, through MEM, assume a leadership role through the implementation of an intersectoral coordination group on rural household energy. MEM participated in the past as the leader of the National Group on Improved Stoves. A coordination group, which should include representation from all key stakeholders, including the Health Ministry and FIS, could have as a mandate the championing and implementation of policies related to meeting the energy needs of rural families. This mandate must be closely linked with broader rural development and poverty reduction programs.

The intersectoral coordination group should make the most of the infrastructure that already exists around the projects that are being implemented. For example, the government should take advantage of the existing structures for promoting stoves, such as FIS, which has distributed more improved stoves than any other entity in Guatemala and has, through its departmental offices, experience and representation in every government *departamento*. Stove-building firms, manufacturers of metal *planchas* and accessories, firms that provide training in the use and maintenance of the stove, and in general the people who have worked in the stove projects also should be brought into the group. It is important that all stakeholders participate in the group and in education and training events for builders and manufacturers, and it is important that they be part of the structure for disseminating stove technology.

NGOs, universities, and other civil society groups also should be participants in the intersectoral coordination group, whether in the promotion and dissemination of the technology, in technical assistance activities related to design or technological diversification, in market and monitoring studies, in promotion, or in the implementation of training and education programs. The intersectoral coordination group should, in summary, coordinate and implement all necessary policy actions directed at meeting the energy needs of rural families.

Technical Unit to Certify Stoves for Subsidy Approval

There is no single agency in Guatemala that can evaluate for the government the quality and efficacy of improved stoves. This situation needs to be rectified. Most successful stoves programs around the world have a government-financed technical unit to evaluate the quality, reliability, and durability of their improved stoves. These units are often involved in testing prototypes to ensure design changes do not come at the expense of performance. Recently some have also begun to assess the health impacts of improved stoves and have started to measure the indoor air pollution consequences of different models. The stove designs that are brought to market should meet efficiency criteria regarding firewood consumption and combustion; and the quality of the stove, its components, materials, and performance also should be certified to protect the user.

It is therefore recommended that the government of Guatemala establish a technical stoves unit to oversee testing and approval of those stoves to be included in programs sponsored by the government and donors. Such a unit could facilitate the work of the coordination group and help to address the weaknesses identified in the historical review of stoves and the three case studies presented here. The technical unit should be coordinated by MEM, but could be run by a third-party NGO or private sector entity. It should include the participation of civil society actors, NGOs, academic institutions, stove users, and international aid agencies, and it should have the support of the government to give it legitimacy in the eyes of these stakeholders.

The technical stoves unit would be responsible for

- research to help develop new stove models and to assist the manufacturers of improved stoves
- verification of the efficiency and quality of the stoves
- market studies (in-house or contracted out) for the different models, to assess and feed back to manufacturers consumer criticism of the products on the market

The principal objective of the technical unit should be diversification of stove models, to give users the ability to select a stove that is appropriate to their needs. Factors to take into consideration include family size, location, the physical characteristics of the user, customs, type of food eaten, and income. To accomplish this the unit would be responsible for coordination at the national level between the various improved stoves projects and programs.

The technical stoves unit would be a focal point for the sharing among programs of information and experiences. It also could provide technical support for projects, helping them with quality control and measurement of the efficiency and pollutant emissions of their stoves. Finally, the unit would protect consumers by evaluating and certifying the general quality of the stoves developed by the producers.

Conclusion

This review of relatively successful projects points the way to important work that must be done for the future development of stoves in Guatemala. First, the subsidy process for improved stoves needs to be more open to encourage innovation—technical and institutional—that can support the promotion of improved stoves. Second, it is essential that a technical stoves unit be established to ensure that the stoves offered to the public are of good design and quality. Not only could energy efficiency be improved and the daily workload of women be reduced, but health and productivity could be improved in rural areas.

The record of the improved stoves program in Guatemala is better than that of any other country in Central America. Between 1996 and 2002 more than 100,000 stoves with metal *planchas* were built in Guatemala, mostly through FIS. The scale of this effort generated national and international interest in the three case studies subsequently undertaken and that are examined here. These studies show that even without a coordinating effort such organizations can succeed in implementing isolated projects. However, Guatemala is now at a stage at which the efforts of these isolated programs should be enhanced by bringing them together within the context of broad rural development and poverty reduction programs, by improving the policy coordination between key stakeholders, by the provision of broad technical support, and by evaluation of the stoves that they individually produce.

Notes

1. The groups are defined as follows: "National Energy Groups are composed of all state and nongovernmental (national and international) institutions that work directly on activities related to the development of renewable energy and also coordinate efforts to provide technical assistance on the most relevant

problems that directly affect the rural and suburban sectors that are held back socially, economically, and technologically. The ultimate objective is integral human development while protecting and conserving the environment" (MEM 1985a).

2. See section on historical review of Improved Stoves Programs in Guatemala.

3. The *plancha armada* was described in an earlier section. In comparison, the cast-iron *plancha* is a cast metal sheet made in one piece. This is usually heavier than the *plancha armada*.

4. The Incó Xanacón Project, carried out by a civil association in the *departamento* of Chiquimula in eastern Guatemala, also did not use doors on the firebox.

5. These suggestions came out of the focus groups conducted by the FIS.

6. According to Manuel Tay, an expert on improved stoves, high-quality *planchas* are not damaged by excessive weight.

5

The Role of LPG

The preceding chapters show that switching entirely to liquefied petroleum gas (LPG) for cooking and heating is one way to substantially reduce, if not eliminate, indoor air pollution due to household fuel use. However, unlike biomass, which may be collected by household members, the use of LPG requires a cash outlay that can be significant for low-income households. This cash outlay includes not only the purchase cost of LPG, but more importantly, the start-up cost of the LPG cylinder and stove. International experience suggests that, even when a government provides support to reduce this start-up cost, the poor often are unable to come up with the cash needed to refill the cylinder to meet their household energy needs.

Because the requirement for cash can make it difficult for low-income households to use LPG, it is important to ensure that end user LPG prices are as close as possible to best practice levels for comparable market environments elsewhere. Economically inefficient high prices will constrain the penetration of LPG into the lower levels of the household market. Whether the end user LPG prices in Guatemala match international best practice levels is therefore an important question to examine. Factors that might contribute to overly high prices could include the following:

- excessive market concentration, leading to possible market control and reduced competition
- fraudulent practices such as the short-selling of LPG, with the result that while the nominal price may seem reasonable the actual price is much higher
- the smuggling of LPG cylinders out of Guatemala to neighboring countries, which would impose excessive costs on the industry and thereby constrain its investment in the new cylinders that are essential to support market growth and penetration

This study assessed the LPG market in Guatemala to gain a better understanding of some of the current and potential future problems that might discourage households from using LPG. To this end it examined market structure, institutional and policy framework, recent price history, and cylinder management.

Fuel Use Patterns

Wood, LPG, and kerosene are the most commonly used household fuels in Guatemala. According to the data obtained in the 2000 Living Standards Measurement Study (LSMS), more than half of the households in Guatemala use a single fuel for cooking and heating—one-third use only wood, and one-fifth use only LPG. Most others use multiple fuels. It is difficult to quantify the use of kerosene because it is used for lighting as well as for cooking and heating, but it appears that its use as a cooking or heating fuel is small. The survey results are summarized in Table 5.1. Data on household income are not available, but household expenditures, including imputed values of items given in kind and those collected for free by household members, are used as a proxy for income. In table 5.1 the households are divided into five expenditure quintiles based on per capita expenditure, with the same number of individuals in each quintile. The top quintile is dominated by urban households, and the bottom quintile by rural households.

In urban areas, close to half of households use only LPG for cooking and heating. As expected, the percentage of LPG-only users increases with increasing expenditure quintile. Among low-expenditure households, wood is the most common fuel, and is used by close to two-thirds of urban households in the bottom two quintiles as their only fuel.

Table 5.1 Household Fuel Use Patterns for Cooking and Heating
percentage of households in each category

Per capita expenditure quintile	LPG only	LPG and kerosene	LPG and wood	LPG, wood, and kerosene	Kerosene only	Kerosene and wood	Wood only
Urban							
1 (poorest)	0.0	0.0	5.9	0.3	1.2	27.8	64.7
2	7.5	0.1	18.1	0.0	0.0	11.2	63.2
3	23.7	0.1	36.0	2.0	0.1	4.3	33.9
4	37.0	0.5	44.5	1.6	0.0	1.4	15.0
5 (richest)	73.2	0.6	22.5	0.7	0.0	0.2	2.7
Urban average	45.4	0.4	30.0	1.1	0.1	3.4	19.6
Rural							
1 (poorest)	0.0	0.0	1.6	0.0	0.0	59.7	38.7
2	0.3	0.0	5.0	1.1	0.1	44.4	49.1
3	1.6	0.2	16.7	2.2	0.0	28.9	50.5
4	5.7	0.0	36.5	5.2	0.0	18.0	34.7
5 (richest)	20.4	0.3	43.0	9.2	0.5	8.2	18.3
Rural average	2.6	0.1	13.6	2.1	0.1	39.4	42.2
National	19.0	0.2	19.9	1.7	0.1	25.6	33.6

Source: Heltberg 2003.

In rural areas, the most common fuel combination among the bottom quintile households is kerosene and wood. However, in many of these households, kerosene is likely used for lighting rather than for cooking and heating, for which wood is the primary fuel. Many of the households that use kerosene and wood may in fact be single-fuel users for the purposes of cooking and heating. Even among households in the top quintile it is more common to supplement LPG with wood than to use exclusively LPG.

Access is an issue with LPG. If there are no LPG dealers in the area, even those households that could otherwise afford LPG cannot use it. Table 5.2

Table 5.2 LPG Availability and Uptake by Households
percentage of households in each category

Parameter	Availability	Uptake	Coverage
National	74	61	45
Urban	98	79	77
Rural	55	37	20
Region			
Metropolitan	96	86	83
North	44	35	15
Northeast	86	53	46
Southeast	71	45	32
Central	87	57	50
Southwest	72	50	36
Northwest	30	46	14
Petén	60	38	23
Poverty			
Nonpoor	91	79	72
All poor	53	25	13
Extreme poor	33	4	1
Per capita expenditure quintile			
1 (poorest)	38	6	2
2	61	29	18
3	80	55	44
4	92	80	74
5 (richest)	98	90	88
Ethnicity			
Nonindigenous	85	69	59
Indigenous	56	42	24
Quiche	73	52	38
Q'eqchi	45	30	14
Kaqchiqel	80	46	37
Mam	32	28	9
Other groups	39	34	13

Source: Foster and Araujo 2001.

shows the availability of LPG in different regions of the country, the uptake rate, and the coverage (availability multiplied by the uptake rate). The vast majority of urban households have access to LPG, compared to only a little more than half of rural households. Less than one-third of households in the northwest region have access to LPG, the lowest of any region in the country. Only one-third of the "extreme poor" live in areas where LPG is available. Access increases with increasing household expenditure, suggesting that the better off tend to live in areas with better infrastructure and enough LPG-purchasing households to justify the establishment of LPG dealerships, while many of the poor are isolated in remote areas. Similarly, some indigenous groups have low access to LPG.

Cost of LPG Consumption

LPG is a gas and needs to be stored under pressure in a cylinder. Cylinder management as a consequence is one of the unique features of LPG trade; it is also what makes the start-up and distribution costs of LPG much higher than the costs for solid or liquid fuels, especially with respect to delivery in rural areas. Even if LPG had the potential of becoming the primary cooking fuel in rural areas, many such areas lack the economies of scale that would permit cylinder distribution, because of their low population density. Furthermore, the probable greater availability of free biomass means that LPG use would likely be lower in rural than in urban areas, again effectively raising the cost of LPG distribution and making it commercially unattractive for potential dealerships.

Most LPG is sold in 25 lb (11.4 kg) cylinders, as shown in Table 5.3. While much smaller cylinders have been marketed to reduce refill costs, international experience with these cylinders is mixed. The most obvious drawbacks of small cylinders include the much higher cost of cylinder management, hence higher unit LPG prices, and the inconvenience of the

Table 5.3 Cylinder Sizes in Guatemala

Cylinder size lb (kg)	Share of cylinder LPG market (%)
20 (9.1)	0.5
25 (11.4)	77.0
35 (15.9)	17.0
40 (18.2)	1.5
60 (27.3)	1.5
100 (45.5)	2.5

Source: Matthews 2002.

need for frequent refills. The latter is a particular disadvantage in areas where cylinder delivery presents logistical problems.

The costs of purchasing an LPG cylinder, accessories, and a stove are shown in Table 5.4. The figures are based on buying the equipment in one cash payment. If the retailer finances the purchase for the buyer over three equal monthly payments, the total cost increases by about 20 to 25 percent. This means, for example, that the two-burner package would, over three payments, cost about US$65.

To illustrate how these costs compare to overall household expenditures, Table 5.5 shows mean monthly expenditures per capita and per household in different quintiles. For the bottom quintile, the start-up cost of about Q 425 (US$54) (after taking the consumer price index into account) is close to two-fifths of the monthly household expenditure. Payment over three installments can amount to one-sixth of the total household expenditure

Table 5.4 Retail Cost of LPG Cylinder and Stove

Item	Quetzales	US$
25 lb (11.4 kg) cylinder, valve/regulator tubing, with about 5–10 lb (2.3–4.6 kg) of LPG	250	31.60
Cylinder, accessories, and gas plus two-burner stove	425	53.80
Cylinder, accessories, and gas plus three-burner stove	470	59.50

Source: Matthews 2002.

Note: Data as of May 2002.

Table 5.5 Mean Monthly per Capita and Household Expenditures
Quetzales

Region	Expenditure	Quintile 1	Quintile 2	Quintile 3	Quintile 4	Quintile 5	Average
Urban	per capita	141	224	326	521	1,588	1,011
	per household	1,056	1,389	1,913	2,590	5,642	3,941
Rural	per capita	132	221	325	497	1,056	363
	per household	975	1,321	1,805	2,140	3,455	1,728
National	per capita	133	222	325	509	1,477	643
	per household	981	1,332	1,839	2,368	5,185	2,685

Source: Heltberg 2003.

Table 5.6 Retail Prices of LPG Sold in 25 lb (11.4 kg) Cylinders, April 22–28, 2002

Location	Quetzales per cylinder
Guatemala City	38.00
Escuintla	44.00
Retalhuleu	42.50
Cobán	42.75
Petén	46.50
Huehuetenango	44.33
Quetzaltenango	40.00
San Marcos	42.33
Chiquimula	40.60
Santa Rosa	41.13
El Progreso	38.00
Zacapa	43.00
Jutiapa	57.83
Jalapa	57.50

Source: Matthews 2002.

Note: 7.83 Quetzales = US$1.00 at the time of the price survey.

per month, exceeding the monthly per capita expenditure. Given that the expenditures calculated here include imputed costs, the percentage of actual cash expenditures would be even higher, especially in rural areas engaged in agriculture.

Retail LPG prices across Guatemala during the last week in April 2002 are shown in Table 5.6. There is about a 50 percent variation in price from region to region, with the lowest prices charged in Guatemala City and El Progreso and the highest in Jutiapa and Jalapa. The rationale for this regional price difference is generally a combination of logistics costs and the different unit costs of storage, bottling, and distribution operations. (Guatemala City, while not the closest location to the main receiving points, is home to by far the largest of these operations.) The degree of market competition may also be a factor in the nature of price differentiation in some locations, but overall is not believed to play a significant role. With the exception of Jutiapa and Jalapa, most upcountry locations had price differentials compared with the capital city of Q2 to Q6 (US$0.25 to US$0.75) per cylinder. Jutiapa and Jalapa are special cases: The LPG market in these locations is small and, because these locations are close to the El Salvador border, most LPG is supplied through smuggling (*contrabando hormiga*), as El Salvador prices are low. The price shown is for the single dealer in each area; this dealer supplies LPG sourced through Guatemalan channels, but in fact sells very little. If the LPG supplies from El Salvador were to be factored into the equation, the effective average price to the public in these two areas would be much lower than the dealer price shown in the table.

Institutional and Regulatory Framework

The regulatory framework for Guatemala's hydrocarbon sector was substantially reformed by the Marketing of Hydrocarbons Law of 1997 and its General Regulation. This legislation includes LPG as a petroleum product and subjects it to the same general health, safety, and environment (HSE) rules as petroleum, as well as to a few special provisions for the licensing of storage, transport and distribution facilities, and operations. No other specific regulatory framework applies to LPG in Guatemala.

According to the legislation, the Guatemalan Commission for Standards (Comisión Guatemalteca de Normas; COGUANOR) is the only government body in Guatemala authorized to prepare and issue norms and standards. However, in practice confusion has arisen due to the fact that various other government entities, including the Ministry of Energy and Mines, are adopting international standards or have put in effect other instruments that they term norms but that frequently are mixtures of technical standards, regulations, and manuals of procedure. According to Article 71 of the Marketing of Hydrocarbons Regulation No. 522 of 1999, the General Directorate of Hydrocarbons (Dirección General de Hidrocarburos; DGH), as the enforcement agency for the hydrocarbon sector, is alone authorized to issue instructions, manuals, and circulars relating to the publication of and compliance with quality specifications, HSE rules, inspection procedures, and other requirements regarding the location, construction, and operation and maintenance of petroleum installations. The relationship between these overlapping rule-making authorities needs to be clarified by legislative action.

The regulatory framework for the petroleum sector in general, and specifically for the LPG supply, consists largely of general references to international standards. In practical terms, the generality of those references makes it nearly impossible for the users as well as the enforcement agency to define the exact rules for each particular case. This creates a high degree of uncertainty for the operators and leaves too much discretion within the inspection and sanctioning process.

In highly developed jurisdictions, such as most of the United States and Europe, as well as a few developing countries, the successful approach has been to issue general regulations that define the institutional attributions, licensing requirements, and enforcement authorities with relatively few technical specifications. Technical specifications are covered by the formal adoption of internationally accepted norms and standards under the respective general legislation. The adoptions are made by specific, rather than general, references to individual standards and codes of practice and include exceptions and other adaptations according to local requirements.

Market Structure and Competitiveness

The LPG market in Guatemala is dominated by the two Mexican Zaragoza family groups TOMZA (Tomás Zaragoza) and ZETA (Miguel Zaragoza). Since early 2001, ZETA has pursued an aggressive business strategy incorporating logistics, pricing, vertical integration, acquisitions, and market penetration. The logistics and market positions of the two dominant companies are so strong that it is difficult to envision the possibility of a new entrant to the market, particularly while ZETA is in the price-cutting mode. In view of these circumstances, the main issue concerning DGH officials is that of excessive market concentration, which has raised the danger of the major players seizing control of the market. The situation has not as yet manifested itself in higher margins and prices, but DGH and the antimonopoly authorities must remain vigilant to the possibility of this happening.

A comparison of LPG small-cylinder prices, exclusive of taxes, in several countries was carried out for this study. As Figure 5.1 shows, LPG prices in Guatemala began to fall sharply in 2002 relative to those of other countries as a result of strong price cutting by ZETA, which set the objective of capturing 75 percent of the Guatemalan market. The imputed margins for supply and distribution of the product to final consumers rank among the lowest in the region.

The retail price of LPG has fallen steadily over this same period, nearly halving between January 2001 and April 2002 as shown in Figure 5.2. If these low margins can be maintained, consumers obviously will benefit. However,

Figure 5.1 Comparison of LPG Prices (exclusive of taxes)

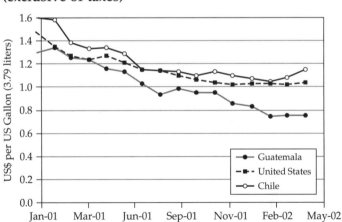

Source: Matthews 2002.

Figure 5.2 Price of LPG Sold in 25 lb (11.4 kg) Cylinder in Guatemala City

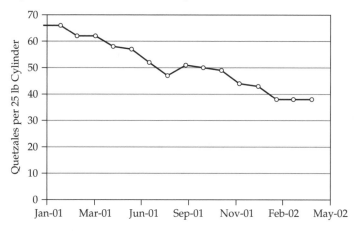

Source: Matthews 2002.

Note: Average exchange rate 7.86 Q = US$1.00 during this period.

if the lower prices are merely a step taken to eliminate the competition, they may represent at best a temporary relief before large price increases follow. Those consumers who have decided in recent months to take up LPG because of its low cost would be especially badly affected by any such price increases.

Commercial Malpractice

The issue of short selling LPG was discussed with DGH officials for this study. The Gas Section (Sección Gas) of the Department of Manufacturing and Distribution (Departamento de Transformación y Distribución) has responsibility for the supply and distribution chain up to and including the filling of cylinders. The Licensing Department (Departamento de Licencias) has the responsibility downstream for this: that is, for cylinder transportation, retailing, and end use. As part of their duties the Sección Gas inspectors do spot checks on cylinder filling equipment and practices. They have seen no major problems at this level, but while it is unrecorded there is a possibility of cylinder "decanting" malpractice downstream of the filling plant. The consumer protection body DIACO (la Dirección de Atención y Asistencia al Consumidor; the Directorate for Consumer Attention and Assistance) of the Ministry of Economy (Ministerio de Economia) is charged with managing this situation as part of its responsibility for surveillance and enforcement of weights and measures. The Licensing Department also deals with issues affecting the LPG household consumer, but these tend to be mainly issues of safety, such as end user equipment setup and practices.

The smuggling of new LPG cylinders out of Guatemala to neighboring countries was not highlighted as a major problem by either DGH officials or by operators in relation to the overall situation of maintenance and renewal of the cylinder stock in general. Some small-scale smuggling (*contrabando hormiga*) occurs of the high-quality "Sherwood" valves rather than of the cylinders themselves; the Sherwood valve is removed and replaced by a lower-quality Chilean or Mexican model.

Safety and Cylinder Management

The existing legislation and regulations provide the DGH with wide-ranging authority and the faculties for supervision, inspection, and sanctions of the supply chain for all products, including LPG. By adopting the principal international standards by specific reference, the DGH could maintain an efficient enforcement system if it had the necessary political support, as well as sufficient staff and technical resources. The staffing and resources of the DGH appear, however, to be insufficient to inspect and control the installations and operations of the LPG supply chain with appropriate frequency and rigor.

The ownership of LPG cylinders in Guatemala has not been established by law, regulation, or by any other means. The total stock of cylinders is estimated to be about 4 million, but neither the number of cylinders in circulation is known with precision nor how much repair and replacement are needed. Any cylinder may be filled at any filling plant regardless of its markings or color (the distribution companies paint their cylinders different colors to create an identity in the marketplace). No rules or any related mechanisms exist for the exchange of cylinders, and no formal exchanges between companies need to take place because cylinder ownership has not been defined. Nor do any rules exist concerning the painting or marking of cylinders for identification purposes. While there are regulations establishing quality and maintenance standards for LPG cylinders, the lack of ownership definition means there is effectively no legal responsibility defined for the maintenance or repair of cylinders and valves.

In the worldwide LPG market there are two principal methods of cylinder ownership: LPG company owned, and customer owned.

Company owned. The company either loans or leases the cylinder to the customer. The customer exchanges an empty cylinder for a full one, paying only for the LPG. The company is responsible for filling and supplying safely maintained cylinders. It is common to have the owner's investment secured through a system of refundable deposits or guarantees in cash.

Customer owned. There are two modalities under this scheme:

- Centralized cylinder filling and distribution. Upon replenishment the customer exchanges a legally owned cylinder for one of like kind. Because the customer does not have physical possession of the cylinder that is brought to the exchange transaction, the customer is not responsible for its replacement at the end of the cylinder's useful life. The LPG supplier has the responsibility of maintenance and replacement, because the initial cylinder is somewhere in the inventory "float."
- Bulk distribution, or "mini filling plant" system. The customer has a personally identified cylinder and brings it to the local filling plant to be refilled when empty. The customer retains the same cylinder through its life and is responsible for its maintenance or replacement. The key to safety in this system is the diligence of the plant operator in inspecting and rejecting as necessary any substandard cylinders. A customer with a substandard cylinder must be refused a filling, unless a new cylinder is purchased. The filling plant or its supplier is responsible for recycling or otherwise disposing of the used cylinder.

Guatemala uses the centralized cylinder filling and distribution system. Elsewhere in the region, Chile and Brazil use the system of company-owned cylinders with refundable deposits. The two countries that use the bulk distribution system and localized filling plants are the United States and Canada.

The system in Chile may offer useful lessons for Guatemala. Among the positive features of the company-owned, refundable-deposit system in Chile are the clear rules and regulations on the interchangeability of cylinders owned by different companies. Each operator is assured of retaining most of its cylinder stock for its own use, thus making it worthwhile for it to spend money from its margin on cylinder rehabilitation and replacement. It is strongly recommended that the government of Guatemala investigate the possibility of converting its cylinder management system to company-owned cylinders, using the Chilean regulatory framework as a model.

Conclusions

There are no obvious market or regulatory distortions in the cylinder LPG market in Guatemala that could be said to be deterring more widespread household use of LPG. In the last few years, steadily falling LPG prices have favored the uptake of LPG, but there has been a worrying increase in the concentration of market power that potentially could result in a reversal of the recent price trend. The government needs to anticipate future changes to prevent the development of a duopoly or monopoly in the sector.

There are indications that some households are paying as much cash to purchase wood or kerosene as they would were they to switch to LPG

(Heltberg 2003). An understanding of why households that seemingly could afford LPG are not yet using it may help expand the LPG market, and thus reduce exposure to indoor air pollution. Finally, a large fraction of the cylinders currently in circulation are estimated to require retirement and renewal in the near future. A better cylinder management system needs to be put in place, for which the regulatory framework in Chile may serve as a useful example.

6

Policy Recommendations

The preceding chapters described the problem of indoor air pollution (IAP) and its links with poverty reduction; provided a ballpark estimate of the extent of this problem in Guatemala; and discussed ways of mitigating the impact of IAP, principally through two interventions: liquefied petroleum gas (LPG) and improved stoves. This chapter draws together the different recommendations and policy options, as well as other topics meriting further discussion, as input for decision makers in Guatemala seeking to address the problem of IAP and its related health impacts.

Poverty and IAP

Chapter 1 showed how IAP in Guatemala is linked with the following:

- *High incidence of poverty*. More than half of all Guatemalans (56 percent, or about 6.4 million people) were living in poverty in 2000.
- *Low levels of rural electrification*. Fewer than 40 percent of the poorest households have electricity connections, compared to 95 percent of the richest households.
- *Large rural population*. More than 60 percent of the Guatemalan population lives in rural areas, including 81 percent of the poor and 93 percent of the extreme poor. Three-quarters of all rural residents fall below the full poverty line, and one-quarter live in extreme poverty.
- *High levels of traditional fuel use*. In Guatemala, fuelwood is the dominant cooking fuel in 97 percent of households in rural areas. Among rural households, 42 percent use fuelwood only, and 55 percent use wood and one or more other types of fuel.

Link with Millennium Development Goals

A growing body of evidence, based on worldwide IAP health studies, indicates that the levels of IAP in homes that use traditional solid fuels are alarmingly high. Exposure monitoring studies in Guatemala confirmed that women and children endure high exposure to toxic pollutants from fuelwood consumption. The worldwide literature also points to a strong association between IAP and health conditions, particularly among children in the first

93

few years of life. Conclusive links between health and IAP are still lacking, but a recently initiated study in the Guatemalan highlands, financed by the U.S. National Institutes of Health, is expected to be an important source of information.

Informal estimates, however, based on the results of worldwide IAP health studies, indicate that the number of annual cases of acute lower respiratory infection (ALRI) in the Guatemalan highlands could be reduced by as many as 24,000, and annual deaths by about 1,000, through the elimination of indoor air pollution. This would be about a 60 percent reduction in the annual cases of ALRI mortality among the 400,000 children under age five who live in households in which open fires are used for cooking.

Despite the lack of conclusive evidence on the extent of health impacts, the general consensus among the broad range of Guatemalan stakeholders represented at the April 2003 workshop was that something has to be done about the problem in the short term. This consensus was reinforced by the fact of the problem's close link with the fourth Millennium Development Goal, related to reducing child mortality, and the fifth goal, related to improving maternal health. This consensus is also consistent with the recommendations of the Guatemala Poverty Assessment Report, which suggest that preventive health measures be emphasized, targeted particularly to the following vulnerable groups: poor and malnourished children, poor women and girls, poor indigenous households, and the rural poor (World Bank 2003). In Guatemala, these groups are also most affected by IAP.

What Can Be Done about Indoor Air Pollution?

International academic journals contain a rich stock of papers on exposure monitoring experiments in Guatemala. The results of some of these are described in chapters 1 and 3. IAP was not a topic on the agenda of any government agency at the start of this project, however. As the study developed, a gradual understanding built, primarily through the dissemination workshops, of the importance of intersectoral collaboration on this issue and of the importance and emotive nature of the issue itself, which is so closely linked with the well-being of children and women, mainly in poor, rural, indigenous households, and with the country's poverty reduction goals. During the April 2003 workshop, participants identified a number of issues as barriers to successfully reducing IAP in rural homes:

- lack of a national policy
- lack of leadership
- apathy (as reflected by a lack of willingness on the part of the government to act and a lack of interest on the part of the population)
- lack of interinstitutional coordination
- resistance to change

- lack of education
- lack of training
- poverty and lack of access to resources
- lack of state policies

These barriers reflect the fact that there is a dire shortage of information about this topic, and as a result no constituency is prepared to act. The interventions described below aim to ensure availability of information so that the extent of the problem can be monitored; facilitate solutions through better coordination and use of technical options; and ensure sustainability in the implementation of options, through the promotion of long-term behavioral change. At a broad level, four types of interventions are needed:

- *Monitoring the problem and improving understanding of the links between health and poverty reduction.* Building a constituency through the provision of information about the subject itself is an important intervention. Strong evidence indicates this problem is closely linked with Guatemala's poverty reduction agenda, but there are gaps in the evidence that need to be filled in. An improved stove intervention trial being conducted by Kirk Smith and his co-workers, which aims to estimate the reduction in ALRI that can be achieved with improved stove use, will shed more light on the severity of the problem of IAP and ALRI in Guatemala and on the effectiveness of improved stoves as an intervention. The government needs to follow this study and other research in this area exploring the link between ALRI and pneumonia and IAP. ALRI and pneumonia are the leading health issues with respect to both morbidity and mortality for children in Guatemala, and a better understanding of these links is important to guide national health policies.
- *Greater interinstitutional coordination.* Greater interinstitutional coordination is probably the most crucial intervention. The issue of IAP is spread across the mandates of different government institutions: for example, the technical mitigation options lie within the mandate of the Ministry of Energy and Mines, but the link with health impacts and dissemination of these impacts lies with the Ministry of Health. In terms of financial resources, the Social Investment Fund (Fondo de Inversíon Social; FIS) has a major role in financing the technical options, such as improved stoves, for poor households. The technical innovation and health impact aspects are missing from its current program, however. This is a case where the sum of the parts clearly would have a greater impact than the cumulative impact of each part separately.

  Coordination of the various stakeholders is also crucial. These stakeholders consist of the government, with which the policy options and the broader mandate of poverty reduction lie; the private sector, which can help develop the market for the technical options, namely improved stoves and liquefied petroleum gas (LPG) in rural areas; nongovernmental organizations (NGOs), which can act as a partner to the government in the implementation of programs addressing health service delivery in rural areas and improved stoves; households, particularly the women who use the stove and the men who choose to buy it and often collect firewood for it; and academia, which is working on establishing a firm link between health and IAP.

A third layer of coordination is with Guatemala's neighbor to the north, Mexico, where 28 million people use firewood for cooking and where the same issues are under discussion. A collaboration across boundaries has great scope for both countries; for example, there are planned and ongoing efforts in Chiapas, a region that shares many cultural and socioeconomic factors with neighboring parts of Guatemala, which could be coordinated with Guatemalan programs. The main advantage of this collaboration would be the creation of a larger market for technical mitigation options, and therefore one that would be more attractive to the private sector. Joint monitoring and research sharing would also bring additional benefits for both countries.

- *Making people aware of the problem to promote behavioral change.* Lack of information and lack of an understanding of the link between smoke and poor health means that there has been no constituency to champion change. The dissemination of the findings of this study has started to build a constituency at the level of the government stakeholders, but much more needs to be done. A striking finding of the stoves study was that women did not see the link between health and smoke. This clearly needs to change if behavioral change is to follow. In one sense, the problem is akin to the improvement of sanitation and its impact on diarrheal diseases. Only after it was recognized that washing hands is crucial to the achievement of a better health outcome (and that the technical option of providing a latrine is not a sufficient condition for this outcome), and after programs accordingly sought to educate mothers on the importance of this realization, did health outcomes improve in sanitation programs.

  Women's groups and NGOs can play an important role in getting the message to the final users. Revising government training and health outreach programs, as well as existing media campaigns for improved stoves and LPG, so that they also discuss the link between smoke and health could greatly help the promotion of long-term changes in behavior.

- *Implementing technical options.* Technical options—principally improved stoves for the lower-income quintiles with targeted subsidies through the FIS, and improved stoves and LPG stoves for the higher-income quintiles—need to be implemented. Most of the existing improved stoves programs (of which there are many compared with other countries in Central America) focus on fuel efficiency, are highly subsidized, offer limited choice to the user, and are implemented in a modular manner, with no interaction between the government and its policies and the different suppliers. The design and implementation of the various programs also seem to follow separate rules. The government must take a more proactive role in establishing policies related to improved stoves programs. It should equally emphasize fuel efficiency and health impact as the key criteria for stove design, and should promote a market-based system that targets subsidies to the poorest and offers choice and training for the user. The implementation of such policies will require full coordination between the different government entities and other nongovernmental stakeholders. Coordination on better house design to improve ventilation is another area for possible government intervention, through building codes and work with local municipal heads. Finally, the government can play a key role in ensuring that the technical options for mitigating IAP are placed firmly in the context of broader rural development programs that seek more generally to reduce poverty. Donors and NGOs also need to ensure that their programs are in step with government efforts and that they are not operating modularly.

The Role of Each Stakeholder in a Solution

IAP is an issue that involves many stakeholders, and for the current situation to change many people must get involved. The technical solutions to the problem are fairly straightforward, but the behavioral and cultural issues are much more important. The participation of the different stakeholders in efforts to promote behavior change is therefore crucial if the solutions are to be sustainable over time. To illustrate this, we present our conclusions from the perspective of the different stakeholders:

President's Office or Ministry of Planning. Without leadership, any activity requiring coordination across institutions is unlikely to succeed. Here, an institution at a different level from the involved ministries, such as the president's office or the Ministry of Finance or Planning, could play an important role in promoting interinstitutional coordination and in bringing mitigation of the impacts of IAP into the context of the country's broader policies and strategies for poverty reduction. The lead institution could also take the reins in the short term by forming a working group of the principal stakeholders to define a plan of action that[1] ultimately could develop into an intersectoral coordination group on rural household energy.

Ministry of Public Health and Social Assistance (MSPAS). This study attempted to estimate the impact of IAP, but more consistent information gathering and monitoring would lead to more accurate monitoring of this issue in Guatemala. In this regard, an expansion of the MSPAS's outdoor pollution unit to include IAP would be a critical step. Given the potential impact of this problem on infant health and mortality and its relation to the national poverty reduction program, the MSPAS could do the following:

- begin to gather better information on this issue, including through influencing the design of subsequent Demographic and Health Survey and Living Standard Measurement Survey questionnaires to retrieve data specifically to help improve understanding of the links between ALRI and pneumonia and IAP
- coordinate with ongoing academic initiatives such as the U.S. National Institutes of Health-financed intervention study
- assist other ministries and the FIS in the design of preventive programs, through participation in an intersectoral coordination group on rural household energy, through the provision of information on the impacts of IAP, by promoting better housing design (to incorporate chimneys and to separate sleeping quarters from the kitchen), and by promoting the mitigation of IAP into broader poverty reduction programs
- take a more active part in disseminating information on IAP in Guatemala by using its clinic outreach program to educate people on ALRI and other health impacts of IAP, such as low birthweight of babies and respiratory problems in women

Ministry of Energy and Mines (MEM). The technical solutions lie predominantly in the hands of the MEM, but the application of many of these solutions requires that this ministry work closely with others, including the Ministries of Planning and Health and the FIS. With respect to the promotion of cleaner household energy options in rural areas, the findings of this study suggest that the MEM could play an important role in establishing an intersectoral coordination group on rural household energy. Such a group should include representatives of all key stakeholders, and should operate with a mandate to champion the implementation of policies related to meeting the energy needs of rural families. It is important that this mandate also be closely linked with broader rural development programs, and that the group's efforts focus on improving existing infrastructure and programs rather than seeking only to create new programs. This applies particularly to the improved stoves programs. Given the high use of fuelwood and its close link with poverty, these programs need to change their current emphasis on large subsidies, which are associated with limited user options and which are focused primarily on fuel efficiency, to more market-based programs that permit the user to choose from a variety of options, and for which health impact and fuel efficiency are the cornerstones of stove design. Efforts also need to be made to educate users on the importance of proper stove maintenance (such efforts should be accompanied by better housing design).

As a complement to the activities of the intersectoral coordination group, the MEM should also establish and lead a technical stoves unit, which would act on behalf of the consumer to certify stove designs and thereby ensure quality, and to encourage the development of a greater range of stoves from which the user could choose.[2] This unit could be run by a third-party NGO or private sector entity. If such a unit were to gain broad acceptance among users, it could be expected that new NGO programs would approach it for certification of their own stove designs; any such engagement of NGOs would encourage research into new designs, would help organize demand from communities, and would support the delivery of services. The government additionally could expand the unit's scope to include non-FIS designs. A final important role of the unit would be to disseminate information to the public, and thereby promote better understanding of the links between health and IAP and further protect users against faulty products.

On the issue of LPG, we have two recommendations for the MEM. First, the ministry needs to closely monitor price movements to ensure that the current duopoly structure in LPG supply does not lead to high end user prices. This is a serious concern given that LPG prices and start-up costs in Guatemala are low by international standards, and market power is concentrated in just two dominant LPG firms. Price and other incentives to promote the use of LPG among the poor must be primarily market-based. Second, the MEM should explore the system of cylinder ownership in which cylinders are owned by firms rather than by individual consumers, thus placing the responsibility for maintaining cylinders and complying with safety regulations with the LPG supplier. A shift to such a system should also accelerate cylinder renewal by minimizing the migration of new cylinders from one firm to another.

Ministry of Environment. Improved stoves are closely linked to greater fuel efficiency and less deforestation. The Ministry of Environment could clearly play a role in an intersectoral coordination group; it could also serve as a member of the board of a technical stoves unit.

Ministry of Foreign Affairs. It is recommended that the Ministry of Foreign Affairs oversee coordination of the IAP issue with Mexico. The advantages of a cross-border collaboration include the creation of a larger market for technical mitigation options—and therefore one that would be more attractive to the private sector—and the related advantages of joint monitoring and sharing of research.

Social Investment Fund (FIS). The FIS is the major supplier of improved stoves in Guatemala. The improved stoves program clearly needs to continue, as better stoves are the primary mechanism for reducing exposure to smoke and IAP. The current FIS program could have a greater impact on reducing the health impacts of IAP through

- providing the user with a choice of certified (for both fuel efficiency and reduced pollution) improved stoves, which would also help to encourage competition in the improved stoves market

- improving training programs on the use and maintenance of stoves by scheduling follow-up sessions for users after they have gained some experience using the stoves
- expanding training to address the links between improved stoves, smoke, and health

The FIS could also play an important part in an intersectoral coordination group and a technical stoves unit by collecting and providing input on how stoves function in the field.

Women's groups. Women's groups could play a crucial role in ensuring the participation and involvement of households and users (who predominantly are women) in the development of a policy on biomass use and in an intersectoral coordination group. In addition, these groups could provide training for women leaders on the hazards of smoke and could collect and provide input on how stoves function in the field.

Private sector stove manufacturers. Manufacturers must work closely with the government to ensure that their products are of an appropriate quality and so they can help convey to users the importance of reducing IAP. In the longer term, this would help improve their own sales. Opening up the FIS to other certified designs would provide an incentive to the manufacturers to move forward along the lines suggested. It would be useful to conduct market studies to clarify the relationship between the market for stoves and subsidies. Such studies would help to inform policy formulation and to define strategies for retail distribution and marketing of stoves. Technical assistance for such studies could be financed by donors through the intersectoral coordination group and the technical stoves unit.

Private sector LPG companies. It is important that LPG suppliers continue their efforts to reach the rural population. More broadly, it is important that they maintain appropriate pricing of LPG and continue to improve cylinder safety. Including an LPG-certified stove with cylinder on the list of stoves offered by the FIS would clearly provide a positive incentive to market development.

NGOs (stoves). It is important that the government of Guatemala build upon and support the considerable base of experience and institutional capacity that has been developed by the stoves programs implemented by NGOs. NGOs need to work closely with the government, ideally through a technical stoves unit, when initiating new programs. It is important that their programs fit in with governmental policy on rural household energy, and that they be focused on the poorest income quintiles. If the FIS should introduce additional certified stove designs, clearly these NGOs could play a role in stove development, in organizing demand, and in delivering service. NGOs also can play a role in providing education to rural communities on the links between improved stoves, IAP, and health; and in collecting information on how well stoves function in the field.

NGOs (health service delivery). Guatemala is unusual in that NGOs play a primary role in providing health services to rural areas. These NGOs, through their contract with the MSPAS, could also help disseminate information on ALRI and other health impacts of IAP to the population.

Academia. The findings from the monitoring literature and field experience attest to the fact that interventions to improve stove efficiency do not necessarily translate to reduced levels of IAP (and notably not of PM_{10}—particulate matter with an aerodynamic diameter less than 10 microns), due to other contributory factors such as housing design and stove maintenance. Further complicating this is the dependence of measured exposure levels on the accuracy and method of measurement. Reducing the variations in measured PM_{10} levels associated with the use of improved stoves, or at least identifying the causes to which these variations may be attributed, is necessary. Detailed and accurate exposure monitoring is clearly required in situations where improved stoves are being used. In particular, background concentration levels of PM_{10} should be monitored and assessments of the effects of these concentrations should be undertaken. Such studies would not only support better understanding of the exposure levels associated with use of improved stoves, but would also provide a better understanding of how improved stoves can be promoted from a health perspective. Moving forward on this type of research, academia needs to work closely with the government, NGOs, and households to ensure that its research findings are incorporated into policy. The role of the intersectoral coordination group will be a key mechanism by which to achieve this.

Foreign donors. Donors play an important role in poverty reduction and in the improved stoves programs. Although they coordinate closely with the government on poverty reduction, coordination on the stoves program has been lax or nonexistent. Such coordination is essential to ensure that the improved stoves programs are appropriately targeted to the neediest, and that they are designed to be sustainable and to have an impact on both fuel use and health.

The budgetary implications of an intervention program cannot be ignored, particularly given the many pressing issues that the Guatemalan government faces. These suggested interventions seek to make current arrangements more efficient and effective in terms of combating IAP, rather than introducing entirely new arrangements. In addition to a more targeted use of existing budgetary resources, additional financing also will be necessary. The new financing would have to cover the establishment of a technical stove unit and an increase in the number of staff in the MSPAS' Environment Unit focused on IAP monitoring and information dissemination. Given the close link between this issue and maternal and child health, it is expected that these increased costs would be offset in the longer term by improvements in health.

The sequencing of some of these events, if these recommendations are followed, is important. For example, the first move by the government would need to be the establishment of the intersectoral coordination group and technical stoves unit. Changes to the FIS program cannot precede this move.

These changes imply a change in the incentive framework under which all IAP stakeholders operate. Opening up the FIS program to more than one design would result in opening up the improved stoves market to several other market players, including regional players; this would increase the options for the user and, in the long term, would bring down the prices of improved stoves. It would also force the stove manufacturers to make more than one design, and would provide an incentive to NGOs to organize demand and to deliver the service. This would be a significant change from the current situation in which the manufacture of each different stove is the sole preserve of a single maker, and in which distinct stove programs are led by NGOs, typically supported by foreign donors. If the FIS were to offer a fixed subsidy amount for all certified improved stoves, the market could provide improved stoves (including LPG stoves) at different price levels, so that the user could make the choice between perhaps an expensive, large stove with a long life (such as the current FIS *plancha*) and a cheaper, small stove with a shorter life for which the FIS subsidy might cover the full cost.

Finally, the activities under this study were chosen to complement existing activities in Guatemala. Therefore, they are by no means comprehensive. The focus of the study has been to provide policy makers with information on the possible extent of the IAP problem in Guatemala. Particular emphasis has been given to policy recommendations to enhance the impact of existing improved stoves and LPG programs. Key areas requiring further investigation include the following:

- research into the changes in exposure to $PM_{2.5}$ (particulate matter with an aerodynamic diameter less than 2.5 microns) of different members of the household when using an improved stove under real conditions (with a focus on operation and maintenance of the stove), and the corresponding impact on health
- analysis of the costs and benefits of different mitigation options
- analysis of LPG availability and corresponding issues in rural areas
- assessment of current and planned rural development programs, and provision of recommendations based on worldwide experience on how best to integrate the technical options for mitigating IAP into the context of these programs

In conclusion, IAP must be made a priority in Guatemala. Despite the many knowledge gaps, there is a strong case that the government and other stakeholders should act to address this issue, in particular because of its close links to child mortality and maternal health.

Notes

1. This suggestion was put forward by one of the working groups in a final dissemination workshop held in Guatemala in April 2003.

2. Including through the FIS program.

Bibliography

Albalak, R., N. Bruce, J. P. McCracken, K. R. Smith, and T. De Gallardo. 2001. "Indoor Respirable Particulate Matter Concentrations from an Open Fire, Improved Cookstove, and LPG/Open Fire Combination in a Rural Guatemalan Community." *Environmental Science Technology* 35(17): 2650–5.

Armstrong, J. R., and H. Campbell. 1991. "Indoor Air Pollution and Exposure and Lower Respiratory Infections in Young Children." *International Journal of Epidemiology* 20(2): 424–8.

Baja Verapaz. 2002. "Technical Report on the Tezulutlán Stove." May. Baja Verapaz, Guatemala.

Boy, E., N. Bruce, and H. Delgado. 2002. "Birth Weight and Exposure to Kitchen Wood Smoke During Pregnancy in Rural Guatemala." *Environmental Health Perspectives* 110(1): 109–14.

Boy, E., N. Bruce, K. R. Smith, and R. Hernández. 2000. "Fuel Efficiency of an Improved Wood-Burning Stove in Rural Guatemala: Implications for Health, Environment, and Development." *Energy for Sustainable Development* IV(2): 23–31.

Bruce, N., L. Neufeld, E. Boy, and C. West. 1998. "Indoor Biofuel Air Pollution and Respiratory Health: The Role of Confounding Factors among Women in Highland Guatemala." *International Journal of Epidemiology* 27(3): 454–8.

Campbell, H., J. R. Armstrong, P. Byass. 1989. "Indoor Air Pollution in Developing Countries and Acute Respiratory Infection in Children." *Lancet* [Letter] 1(8645): 1012.

CEMAT (Centro Mesoamericano de Estudios sobre Tecnología Apropiada). 1990. "Estudio de Mercado de Estufas de Leña en el Área Metropolitana de Guatemala." Guatemala.

Cerqueiro, M. C., P. Murtagh, A. Halac, M. Avila, and M. Weissenbacher. 1990. "Epidemiological Risk Factors for Children with Acute Lower Respiratory Tract Infection in Buenos Aires, Argentina: A Matched Case Control Study." *Review of Infectious Diseases* 12 (Suppl 8): S1021–8.

Collings, D. A., S. D. Sithole, and K. S. Martin. 1990. "Indoor Woodsmoke Pollution Causing Lower Respiratory Disease in Children." *Tropical Doctor* 20(4): 151–5.

Cruz, J. A., E. A. González, C. Quintero, and L. Larios. 1997. "Prevalencia de Bronquitis Crónica, Asthma y Sintomatología Respiratoria Asociada a la Exposición de Humo de Leña en la Población Urbana de León" ("Prevalence of Chronic Bronchitis, Asthma and Respiratory Symptoms Associated with Exposure to Fuelwood Smoke in the Urban Population of León"). León, Nicaragua: Universidad Nacional Autónoma de Nicaragua, Facultad de Ciencias Médicas.

Dantzker, D., and S. Scharf. 2000. *Cuidados Intensivos Cardiopulmonares (Intensive Cardiopulmonary Care)* (Tercera Edición en Español). McGraw-Hill Interamericana.

de Francisco, A., J. Morris, A. J. Hall, J. R. M Armstrong Schellenberg, and B. M. Greenwood. 1993. "Risk Factors for Mortality from Acute Lower Respiratory Tract Infections in Young Gambian Children." *International Journal of Epidemiology.* 22(6): 1174–82.

ESMAP (Energy Sector Management Assistance Program)/World Bank. 2000. "Indoor Air Pollution: Energy and Health for the Poor." Washington, DC: ESMAP/World Bank.

Ezzati, M., and D. M. Kammen. 2001a. "Indoor Air Pollution from Biomass Combustion and Acute Respiratory Infections in Kenya: An Exposure-Response Study." *Lancet* 358(9282): 619–24.

———. 2001b. "Quantifying the Effects of Exposure to Indoor Air Pollution from Biomass Combustion on Acute Respiratory Infections in Developing Countries." *Environmental Health Perspectives* 109(5): 481–8.

Ezzati, M., H. Saleh, and D. M. Kammen. 2000. "The Contributions of Emissions and Spatial Microenvironments to Exposure to Indoor Air Pollution from Biomass Combustion in Kenya." *Environmental Health Perspectives* 108(9): 833–9.

Filmer, D., and L. Pritchett. 1998. "Estimating Wealth Effects without Expenditure Data—or Tears: An Application to Educational Enrollments in the States of India." Washington, DC: World Bank.

Foster, V., and C. Araujo. 2001. "Poverty and Modern Utility Services in Guatemala." Background paper for World Bank (2003) *Guatemala Poverty Assessment Report* (No. 24221-GU). Washington, DC: World Bank.

Fundación Solar. 2002. *Estudio de Evaluación de Programas de Estufas Mejoradas en Guatemala*, September.

Fundación Solar. 2002. "Evaluation of Improved Stove Programs in Guatemala." ESMAP (Energy Sector Management Assistance Program) background paper. Washington, DC: World Bank.

Gragnolati, M., and A. Marini. 2003. "Health and Poverty in Guatemala." Latin America and Caribbean Region Policy Research Working Paper 2966. Washington, DC: World Bank.

Heltberg, R. 2003. "Guatemala: Household Fuel Use and Fuel Switching." ESMAP (Energy Sector Management Assistance Program) Technical Paper 036. Washington, DC: World Bank.

Hughes, G., K. Lvovsky, and M. Dunleavy. 2001. "Environmental Health in India: Priorities in Andhra Pradesh." Environment and Social Development Unit, South Asia Region. World Bank.

ICADA CHOQUI, CEMAT, XELAC. 1980. "Memoria Segundo Encuentro Nacional de Tecnología Apropiada: Estufas de Lorena." Guatemala.

INE (Instituto Nacional de Estadística). 1994. "Guatemala. X Censo de Población y V de Habitación 1994." Available at *http://www.segeplan. gob.gt/ine/index.htm* as of September 2002.

Johnson, A. W., and W. I. Aderele. 1992. "The Association of Household Pollutants and Socio-Economic Risk Factors with the Short-Term Outcome of Acute Lower Respiratory Infections in Hospitalised Pre-School Nigerian Children." *Annals of Tropical Paediatrics* 12(4): 421–32.

Klein, J. P., and M. L. Moeschberger. 1997. *Survival Analysis: Techniques for Censored and Truncated Data*. New York: Springer Verlag.

Kossove, D. 1982. "Smoke-Filled Rooms and Lower Respiratory Disease in Infants." *South African Medical Journal* 61(17): 622–4

Lou Ma, R., and L. Silvia Sánchez. 1983. "Producción Masiva y Normalizada de Pequeñas Estufas de Leña para el Área Rural de Guatemala." Guatemala: Centro de Experimentación de Tecnología Apropiada (CETA).

Macro International. 1999. *Guatemala: Encuesta Nacional de Salud Materno Infantil 1998–1999 (Guatemala: National Maternal and Infant Health Survey 1998–1999)*. Instituto Nacional de Estadística (INE), Ministerio de Salud Pública y Asistencia Social (MSPAS), USAID, UNICEF, UNFPA, Macro International Inc. Calverton, Maryland.

Martinez Cuellar, M. 2003. "La Demanda por Combustible y el Impacto de la Contaminacion al Interior de los Hogares Sobre la Salud: El Caso de Guatemala." Documento Cede, 2003–2006. Bogotá: Universidad de los Andes.

Matthews, W. 2002. "LPG for Household Use in Guatemala." Consultant report submitted to the World Bank.

McCracken, J. P., and K. R. Smith. 1998. "Emission and Efficiency of Improved Wood Burning Cook Stoves in Highland Guatemala." *Environment International* 24(7): 739–47.

McCracken, J. P., R. Albalak, E. Boy, N. Bruce, J. Hessen, M. A. Schei, and K. R. Smith. 1999. "Improved Stove or Interfuel Substitution for Decreasing Indoor Air Pollution from Cooking with Biomass Fuels in Highland Guatemala." *Indoor Air* 3: 118–23.

Mendoza, I., and E. Boy. 1993. "Contaminación Intra Domiciliaria con Monóxido de Carbono del Humo de Leña en Viviendas del Área Rural de Guatemala". Guatemala City: Instituto de Nutrición de Centro América y Panamá (INCAP).

MEM (Ministerio de Energía y Minas de Guatemala). 1985a. "Propuesta de Capacitación del Grupo Nacional de Estufas Mejoradas." Guatemala City.

———. 1985b. "Memoria del Tercer Encuentro Nacional de Estuferos." Guatemala City.

———. 1985c. "Informe de la Encuesta Nacional de Estufas Mejoradas en Guatemala." Grupo Nacional de Estufas Mejoradas. Guatemala City.

———. 1988. "Estudio de Base para el Diseño de Estufas Mejoradas para las Tortillerías de la Ciudad Capital." Sección de Leña y Carbón Vegetal. Guatemala City.

———. 2001. "Estufas Mejoradas de Leña en Guatemala. Unidad de Planificación." Guatemala City.

Ministerio de Salud Publica y Asistencia Social. 2001. "Indicadores Básicos de Salud en Guatemala." Guatemala City.

Mtango, F. D., D. Neuvians, C. V. Broome, A. W. Hightower, and A. Pio. 1992. "Risk Factors for Deaths in Children under 5 Years Old in Bagamoyo District, Tanzania". *Tropical Medicine and Parasitology* 43(4): 229–33.

Murray, C. J. L., and A. D. López. 1996. *Global Burden of Disease.* Cambridge, Mass.: Harvard University Press.

Naeher, L. P., B. P. Leaderer, and K. R. Smith. 2000. "Particulate Matter and Carbon Monoxide in Highland Guatemala: Indoor and Outdoor Levels from Traditional and Improved Wood Stoves and Gas Stoves." *Indoor Air* 10(3): 200–5.

Naeher, L. P., K. R. Smith, B. P. Leaderer, D. Mage, and R. Grajeda. 1999. "Spatial Particle Mass and Carbon Monoxide Indoor and Outdoor Concentrations in Relation to Sources in High and Low Density Housing in Rural Guatemala". In Proceedings of Indoor Air '99: The Eighth International Conference on Indoor Air Quality and Climate." Edinburgh, Scotland. *Indoor Air* 3: 124–9.

———. 2000. "Indoor and Outdoor $PM_{2.5}$ and CO in High- and Low-Density Guatemalan Villages." *Journal of Exposure Analysis and Environmental Epidemiology* 10 (6 Pt. 1): 544–51.

Naeher, L. P., K. R. Smith, B. P. Leaderer, L. Neufeld, and D. T. Mage. 2001. "Carbon Monoxide as a Tracer for Assessing Exposures to Particulate Matter in Wood and Gas Cookstove Households of Highland Guatemala." *Environmental Science and Technology* 35(3): 575–81.

National Council for Population and Development. 1993. *"Demographic and Health Survey–Kenya. 1993."* Macro International Inc., Calverton, Maryland. Available at *http://www4.worldbank.org/afr/poverty/databank/survnav/show_survey.cfm?ID=80* as of September 2002.

Neufeld, L. 1995. "The Influence of Smoke from Indoor Cooking Fires on Haemoglobin Concentration in Women from Rural Highland Guatemala." (Masters thesis.) Ithaca, New York: Cornell University.

O'Dempsey, T., T. F. McArdle, J. Morris, N. Lloyd-Evans, I. Balden, B. Laurence, E. Secka, and B. M. Greenwood. 1996. "A Study of Risk Factors for Pneumococcal Disease among Children in a Rural Area of West Africa." *International Journal of Epidemiology* 25(4): 885–93.

Pandey, M., R. Neupane, A. Gautam, and I. Shrestha. 1989. "Domestic Smoke Pollution and Acute Respiratory Infections in a Rural Community of the Hill Region of Nepal." *Environment International* 15: 337–40.

Restrepo, J., P. Reyes, P. de Ochoa, and E. Patiño. 1983. "Neumoconiosis por Inhalación del Humo de Leña." *Revista Acta Médica Colombiana* 8: 191–204.

Riojas-Rodríguez, H., P. Romano-Riquer, C. Santos-Burgoa, and K. R. Smith. 2001. "Household Firewood Use and the Health of Children and Women of Indian Communities in Chiapas, Mexico." *International Journal of Occupational and Environmental Health* 7(1): 44–53.

Shah, N., V. Ramankutty, P. G. Premila, and N. Sathy. 1994. "Risk Factors for Severe Pneumonia in Children in South Kerala: A Hospital Based Case-Control Study." *Journal of Tropical Pediatrics* 40(4): 201–6.

Smith, K. R. 1999. "Indoor Air Pollution." Environment Department, Pollution Management in Focus Discussion Note 4. Washington, DC: World Bank.

————. 2000. "National Burden of Disease in India from Indoor Air Pollution." *Proceedings of the National Academy of Sciences* 97(24): 13286–93.

Smith, K. R., J. M. Samet, I. Romieu, and N. Bruce. 2000. "Indoor Air Pollution in Developing Countries and Acute Lower Respiratory Infections in Children." *Thorax* 55(6): 518–32.

Smith, K. R., Y. Lui, J. Rivera, E. Boy, B. Leaderer, C. S. Johnston, Y. Yanagisawa, and K. Lee. 1993. "Indoor Air Quality and Child Exposures in Highland Guatemala." In J. J. K. Jaakkola, ed., *Indoor Air 1993* 1: 441–6. Helsinki: University of Technology.

Torres, J. E. 2002. "Does Fuelwood Smoke Endanger Infant Health? Evidence from DHS and LSMS Surveys in Guatemala." Draft ESMAP (Energy Sector Management Assistance Program) Background Paper. Washington, DC: World Bank.

Victora, G. G., S. C. Fuchs, J. A. Flores, W. Fonseca, and B. Kirkwood. 1994. "Risk Factors for Pneumonia Among Children in a Brazilian Metropolitan Area." *Pediatrics* 93(6): 977–85.

VITA (Voluntarios en Asistencia Técnica). 1980. "Para Qué Sirve Su Estufa de Lorena, Cómo Hacer Su Estufa de Lorena, Cómo Usar Su Estufa de

Lorena." Quetzaltenango, Guatemala: Investigaciones Científicas Asociadas del Altiplano.

————. 1982. *Diccionario de Energía Renovable.*

Von Schirnding, Y., N. Bruce, K. R. Smith, G. Ballard-Tremeer, M. Ezzati, and K. Lvovsky. 2001. "Addressing the Impact of Household Energy and Indoor Air Pollution on the Health of the Poor: Implications for Policy Action and Intervention Measures." WHO (World Health Organization) Commission on Macroeconomics and Health, CMH Working Paper Series, Paper No. WG5:12. Geneva: WHO. Available at *http://www.cmhealth.org/docs/wg5_paper12.pdf*

Wang, L. 2001. "Health Outcomes in Poor Countries and Policy Options: A Summary of Empirical Findings from the DHS Data." Environment Department. Washington, DC: World Bank.

Westhoff, B., and D. Germann. 1995. *Estufas en Imágenes.* Comisión de las Comunidades Europeas. Brussels, Belgium.

WHO (World Health Organization). 2002. *The World Health Report 2002: Reducing Risks, Promoting Healthy Life.* Geneva: World Health Organization.

World Bank. 1999. *Fuel for Thought: Environmental Strategy for the Energy Sector.* Washington, DC: World Bank.

————. 2003. "Poverty in Guatemala." Guatemala Poverty Assessment Report. Report No. 24221-GU. Washington, DC: World Bank.

World Bank/INE/UN (World Bank, Instituto Nacional de Estadística, United Nations). 2000. *Encuesta Nacional sobre Condiciones de Vida 2000–ENCOVI 2000 (2000 National Survey of Living Conditions).* World Bank, Washington, DC.

Zhang, J., and K. R. Smith. 1996. "Hydrocarbon Emissions and Health Risks from Cookstoves in Developing Countries." *Journal of Exposure Analysis and Environmental Epidemiology* 6(2): 147–61.

Index

Figures, tables, and notes are indicated by f, t, and n.

academic role, recommendations
    for, 101
acute respiratory infections
    (ARIs) and acute lower
    respiratory infections
    (ALRIs), xx, 1, 10*n*1, 28–29
    associated with IAP, 7, 29,
      34–37, 36*t*, 42–48*t*
    in Guatemalan highlands,
      xvi, 37, 38–39*t*, 40–41
    children under age of five. *See*
      children's exposure to
      indoor air pollution
    epidemiological studies relating
      IAP to, 42–48*t*
    exposure monitoring and, 3*t*,
      3–7, 5–6*t*, 95
    fuelwood smoke exposure and,
      11, 17, 21, 23, 24*t*, 25,
      26, 27
    LPG and, 23, 24*t*, 25–26
    shared-use kitchens and, 21, 23,
      24*t*, 25–26
armada planchas. See planchas
    (wood-burning stoves with
    chimneys)

Baja Verapaz. *See* Tezulutlán stove
    project
behavioral changes needed. *See*
    cultural and behavioral
    factors

cancer. *See* lung cancer
carbon monoxide (CO)
    infants' exposure, 21
    open fires vs. *planchas* vs. LPG
      stoves, 4–6, 6*t*
cataracts and solid fuel use, 29
certification of stoves, technical
    unit needed for, xix, 78–79
charcoal use, 31
children's exposure to indoor air
    pollution
    under age five, health impact,
      xvi, 1–2, 8, 28–48
    carbon monoxide exposure, 21
    fuel use and, 1–2, 21–26
      DHS study, 23, 24*t*
      LSMS study, 25*t*, 25–26
    infant deaths from ARIs, 3, 11, 17
    infant respiratory illness, 21,
      23–26
    parental education levels and
      child health and infant
      survival, 16
    particulate matter exposure, 1,
      34, 41, 46
    poverty reduction efforts and, 7
    socioeconomic factors in,
      14–16, 15*t*
Chile's LPG system, 90
chimneys
    See also planchas (wood-burning
      stoves with chimneys)

children's respiratory problems and, 23, 26
frequency of, 21
positive effect of, 2
problems reported with, 65, 68, 68*t*
rural areas, 30, 31
China and open coal stove use, 29
chronic obstructive pulmonary disease (COPD), 1, 29
CO. *See* carbon monoxide
coal stoves, 29
COGUANOR (Comisión Guatemalteca de Normas, Guatemalan Commission for Standards), 87
commercial production and marketing of cooking stoves, 53–55
consumer protection and LPG sales, 89–90
context of study, 8
contrabando hormiga. See smuggling of LPG cylinders
cooking fuel use, 17–21, 18*t*, 20*t*
See also specific type of fuel
in Guatemalan highlands, 30–34, 31*t*, 33*t*
respiratory health and, 21–26
DHS study, 23–24
LSMS study, 25*t*, 25–26
coordination. *See* interagency coordination needed
cost of interventions, xix, 63
See also subsidies for improved stoves programs
cultural and behavioral factors
in improved stoves programs, 72
in improving indoor air quality, xiii, xviii, 2, 96

death. *See* morbidity and mortality
Demographic and Health Survey (DHS), xv, 9, 11–27

scope of, 12, 13*t*
socioeconomic profile, 14, 16
types of fuel used, 17, 18*t*, 19, 30–31, 31*t*
respiratory health in children and, 23, 24*t*
design of stoves. *See* improved stoves programs
DIACO (la Dirección de Atención y Asistencia al Consumidor; Directorate for Consumer Attention and Assistance) and LPG sales, 89
Dirección General de Hidrocarburos (DGH, General Directorate of Hydrocarbons), 87, 88, 89, 90
disability-adjusted life years (DALYs), 2, 10*n*2
disability due to indoor air pollution exposure, 1–2, 29
See also acute respiratory infections (ARIs) and acute lower respiratory infections (ALRIs)
dual-fuel households, 19, 21, 26, 27, 31

electricity
availability and use of, 16, 17, 17*t*
Guatemalan highlands, use in, 31
mitigating effect on IAP, 2, 2*f*
rural electrification, low levels of, xiv, 7, 93
Encuesta Nacional sobre Condiciones de Vida 2000, 14
Energy Sector Management Assistance Program (ESMAP), xiv, 8, 9
environmental tobacco smoke (ETS), 1, 8

epidemiological studies relating
  indoor air pollution to
  acute respiratory
  infections, 42–48*t*
estimating health impact, 9, 28–48
  See also children's exposure to
  indoor air pollution;
  women's exposure to
  indoor air pollution
  acute lower respiratory
  infections, 28–29
  associated with IAP,
  calculation of, 37, 38–39*t*,
  40, 42–48*t*
  children under age five, xvi,
  1–2, 28–48
  in Guatemalan highlands,
  30–34, 33*t*
  of IAP, 9, 34–37, 36*t*, 42–48*t*
  morbidity and mortality. *See*
  morbidity and mortality
  particulate matter. *See*
  particulate matter
  exposure
  scope of study, 28–30
  types of fuel used, 1–2, 2*f*, 3–7,
  30–34, 31*t*
European Union (EU) financing of
  stoves program, 57, 58
  See also Tezulutlán stove project

fire. *See* open fires
FIS. *See* Social Investment Fund
  (FIS, Fondo de Inversión
  Social)
FODIGUA (Fund for Indigenous
  Development), 55
FONAPAZ (National Fund for
  Peace), 55
foreign donors, recommendations
  for, 101
*Fuel for Thought: Environmental
  Strategy for the Energy
  Sector* (World Bank), xiv, 8

fuels
  See also cooking fuel use; *specific
  types of fuel*
  cleaner, xiii, 2, 7, 19, 21, 23,
  26, 27
  mitigation of IAP and, 2, 2*f*, 9
  renewable energy
  applications, 50
  respiratory health of children
  and, 21–26
  sources of, 1
  traditional fuel use, high levels
  of, xiv, 7, 27, 93
  use patterns, 17, 18*t*, 19, 82–83*t*,
  82–84
fuelwood
  ARIs and, 23, 24*t*, 25, 26, 27
  combined with clean fuel use.
  See dual-fuel households
  cost of, 91–92
  fuel use patterns, 17, 82*t*, 82–84
  infant morbidity and mortality
  and, 17
  Intervida wood-saving stove
  project, 60–61
  rural communities, use in, 17,
  19, 27, 31, 31*t*
  as traditional fuel, xiv, 7, 27, 93
  urban communities, use in, 19, 27
  women, use by, 21
Fundación Solar, 55
Fund for Indigenous Development
  (FODIGUA), 55
future research needs, xx, 9, 27,
  102–103

Gas Section (Sección Gas) of the
  Department of
  Manufacturing and
  Distribution
  (Departamento de
  Transformación y
  Distribución) role with
  LPG, 89

General Directorate of
    Hydrocarbons (Dirección
    General de Hidrocarburos,
    DGH), 87, 88, 89, 90
Guatemalan Commission for
    Standards (Comisión
    Guatemalteca de Normas,
    COGUANOR), 87
Guatemalan highlands
    children and IAP, xvi, 8, 30–48
    individual exposure
        estimation, 34
    types of cooking fuels used,
        30–34, 31t, 33t
Guatemalan ministries. *See*
    headings starting with
    "Ministry"
Guatemala Poverty Assessment
    Report (World Bank 2003),
    xvi, 7–8, 9

health impacts. *See specific disease*
    or illness
    estimating. *See* estimating
        health impact
    for particulate matter. *See*
        particulate matter exposure
    respiratory infection. *See* acute
        respiratory infections
        (ARIs) and acute lower
        respiratory infections
        (ALRIs)
heart disease in women and solid
    fuel use, 29
highlands. *See* Guatemalan
    highlands
household energy use, 17–21, 18t,
    20t, 22t
    See also cooking fuel use
hydrocarbon regulation. *See* lique-
    fied petroleum gas (LPG)

IAP. *See* indoor air pollution (IAP)
    and health

ICADA Choquí Experimental
    Station, 50
improved stoves programs,
    xviii–xix, 49–80
    See also Intervida program;
        Social Investment Fund
        (FIS, Fondo de Inversión
        Social); Tezulutlán stove
        project
    age of stove, effect of, 65, 68t
    certification of stoves, technical
        unit needed for, xix, 78–79
    communication and
        promotion, 56
    institutional and participant
        roles for promoting stoves,
        77–78
    customer service and
        satisfaction, 56
    design, xx, 54f, 60f, 62f, 65f
    after-sales maintenance and
        other quality issues, 53,
        64–66, 65f, 67–68t, 74
    interaction between stove
        users, builders, and
        designers, 70–72, 77, 97
    development history of
        improved stoves,
        49–55, 51t
    period of decline, 52–53
    promotion of commercial
        models, 53–55
    technological innovation,
        1976–1980, 50
    financing of program, 56, 63
    gas stoves, effect of use of, 5
    interagency coordination
        needed for, xvii, 74, 77, 95
    local perception of stoves, 57
    manufacturers' role, recommen-
        dations on, xx, 100
    marketing and, 56, 76–77
    operational procedure, 56
    pricing of stoves, xix, 56, 63, 72

improved stoves programs (*cont.*)
  recommendations and lessons,
    74, 76–79, 100
  research studies on, 55–57, 56*t*
  comparative assessment of,
    63–72
  positive features of, 72–73,
    73*t*
  weaknesses of, 74, 75*t*
  subsidies needed for rural
    consumers, 63–64, 64*t*, 74,
    76, 78–79
  technical assistance issues, 74
  user perceptions of improved
    stoves, 66, 68–70, 69*t*
Incó Xanacón Project, 80*n*4
indoor air pollution (IAP) and
    health, xiii, 11–27
  See also particulate matter
    exposure
  acute lower respiratory
    infections. *See* acute
    respiratory infections
    (ARIs) and acute lower
    respiratory infections
    (ALRIs)
  barriers to improving air quality,
    xviii, 2
    See also policy
    recommendations
  effects of, xv–xvi, 1, 11, 29, 39*t*
  estimation of, 34–37, 36*t*,
    42–48*t*
  epidemiological studies relating
    to acute respiratory
    infections, 42–48*t*
  fuels and, 1–2, 3–7, 29
    See also specific type of fuel
  in Guatemalan highlands, 8,
    30–34
  household energy use and,
    17–21, 18*t*, 20*t*, 22*t*
  infant respiratory illness
    analysis and national
    surveys, 21, 23–26, 27

DHS study evidence, 9, 14,
    23–24, 24*t*
  LSMS study evidence, 9, 25*t*,
    25–26
  kitchen type and ventilation, 21,
    22*t*, 23, 25–26, 30
  mitigation methods, effective-
    ness of, 2, 2*f*, 9
  nature of problem, 3–8
  policy recommendations for,
    xvi–xvii, 94–97
  poverty and. *See* poverty and
    indoor air pollution
  socioeconomic profile, 14,
    16–17, 17*t*
  study limitations, 26–27
  survey samples, 12–14
  DHS sample, 9, 12, 13*t*
  LSMS sample, 12–14, 15*t*
infants. *See* children's exposure to
    indoor air pollution
interaction among stove users,
    builders, and designers,
    importance of, 70–72
interagency coordination needed,
    xvii, 74, 77, 95
Intervida program, 57, 59–61, 60*f*,
    63, 71–72
  See also improved stoves
    programs

Kenya and particulate matter
    exposure, 34, 35–37,
    36*t*, 41*n*4
kerosene
  cost of, 91–92
  fuel use patterns, 17, 18*t*, 19, 31,
    82*t*, 82–84
  mitigation of IAP and, 2
kitchen type, 21, 22*t*, 23, 25–26, 30

Licensing Department
    (Departamento de
    Licencias) role with LPG,
    89–90

liquefied petroleum gas (LPG), 9,
    81–92
  ARIs and, 23, 24*t*, 25–26
  commercial malpractice of short
    selling, 89–90
  comparison with open fires and
    planchas, 6, 6*t*
  cost of using, 81, 84–87, 85–86*t*,
    88*t*, 88–89, 91–92
  cylinder safety and
    management, 84*t*, 84–85,
    89, 90–91
  fuel use patterns and, xx, 17,
    18*t*, 82–83*t*, 82–84
  future research needs, 9
  Guatemalan highlands, use in, 31
  market structure and
    competitiveness, 82–83*t*,
    88–89, 88–89*f*
  mitigation methods,
    effectiveness of, 2, 2*f*
  recommendations on private
    companies' role, 100
  regulatory framework for, 87
  short-selling of, 81, 89
  smuggling of LPG cylinders, 81,
    86, 90
Living Standards Measurement
    Study (LSMS), xv, 9, 11–27
  fuel use and respiratory health
    in, 25*t*, 25–26
  Guatemalan highlands data
    from, 30–31
  measuring factors associated
    with IAP in, 17
  scope of, 12, 14, 15*t*
  types of fuel used, 17, 19, 20*t*,
    30–31
Lorena stove, 3, 50, 51*t*, 52
  See also improved stoves
    programs
lung cancer, 1, 29

Marketing of Hydrocarbons Law
    of 1997, 87

Mesoamerican Exchange on
    Efficient Cooking
    Techniques and Improved
    Stoves, 55
metal (*armada*) used in *planchas*.
    See planchas (wood-
    burning stoves with
    chimneys)
Mexico, coordination with,
    xviii, 96
Millennium Development Goals,
    xv–xvi, 8, 93–94
Ministry of Energy and Mines
    (MEM)
  FIS program adopting stove
    designed by, 55
  National Group for Improved
    Stoves, 52, 53, 77
  policy recommendations for,
    xix, xvii, 98–99
  standards adoption by, 87
  training program for building
    stoves, 54
Ministry of Environment, role
    of, 99
Ministry of Foreign Affairs, role
    of, 99
Ministry of Planning, role of, 97
Ministry of Public Health and
    Social Assistance (MSPAS),
    role of, 97–98
mitigation methods, effectiveness
    of, 2, 2*f*, 9
morbidity and mortality, 1–2, 7
  causes in Guatemala
    (1997–2000), 3*t*
  infants and children, xvi, 3, 17,
    23, 26, 34, 37, 40

National Fund for Peace
    (FONAPAZ), 55
National Group for Improved
    Stoves, 52, 53, 77
National Institutes of Health (U.S.)
    study, 6, 9, 94

National Survey of Improved
    Stoves, 52
nature of problem, xiii, xiv, xvii, 3t,
    3–8, 5t, 6t
Nicaragua and fuelwood use, 11, 19
nongovernmental organizations
    (NGOs)
    dissemination role of, xviii,
        77, 96
    health initiatives, recommenda-
        tions for, 101
    improved stoves programs,
        involvement recommended,
        76, 78–79, 100–101
    Intervida program role of. See
        Intervida program
    Tezulutlán project role of, 58–59

Office of Alternative and
        Renewable Energy, 52
open fires
    carbon monoxide and, 4–5
    Guatemalan highlands, use
        in, 31
    morbidity and mortality of
        children and, 37, 40
    particulate matter levels from.
        See particulate matter
        exposure
    planchas compared, 4–6, 6t
    respiratory effects of. See acute
        respiratory infections
        (ARIs) and acute lower
        respiratory infections
        (ALRIs)
    reversion of household to, 63
outdoor kitchens, 21

particulate matter exposure, xx, 1,
        30–34, 33t
    future research needs, 9
    individual exposure estimation,
        4–5, 34, 35–37, 36t
    open fires vs. planchas and, 4–6,
        6t, 32–34, 33t, 41

planchas (wood-burning stoves
        with chimneys)
    See also improved stoves
        programs
    armada (metal components),
        53–54, 61–62, 62f, 64–65,
        71, 80n3
    background of, 49–50, 51t
    carbon monoxide, 4–5
    development of, 49
    FIS stove, 61–62, 62f, 63, 65f
    Guatemalan highlands,
        use in, 31
    innovations to, 55, 77–78
    mejoradas (improved), 32,
        33t, 41n2
    models of, 54f, 60f, 62f, 65f
    morbidity and mortality and, 37
    open fires compared, 4–6, 6t
    particulate matter exposure
        and, 4–6, 32–34, 41
    problems with, 64–70, 67–68t
    user perceptions of, 68, 70
$PM_{2.5}$ and PM_{10}. See particulate
        matter exposure
pneumonia, 1, 7, 29
    See also acute respiratory
        infections (ARIs) and acute
        lower respiratory infections
        (ALRIs)
policy recommendations, xvi–xvii,
        93–109
    key stakeholders' roles, 97–103
    Millennium Development Goals
        and, xv–xvi, 93–94
    targeting poverty, 7–8, 93
poverty and indoor air pollution
    extreme poverty line, definition
        of, 10n3
    full poverty line, definition of,
        10n4
    high incidence of, xiv, 7, 93
    reduction efforts, targeting, xvii,
        7–8, 93
    socioeconomic profile, 14

Poverty Assessment Report (World Bank 2003), xvi, 7–8, 9
President's Office, role of, 97
pricing of stoves, xix, 56, 63, 72
promotion of improved stoves, 53–55, 56
  institutional and participant roles for, 77–78
propane stoves, 53

Quetzaltenango area. See Guatemalan highlands

recommendations. See policy recommendations
respiratory infections. See acute respiratory infections (ARIs) and acute lower respiratory infections (ALRIs)
rural communities
  See also Guatemalan highlands; improved stoves programs
  dual-fuel households, 19
  electrification, low levels of, xiv, 7, 17, 18t
  fuelwood use, 17, 18t, 19, 31, 83
  future research needs, 9
  harmful exposure in, 1, 7, 21, 22t
  improved stoves programs and, 57, 58–59, 59f
  kerosene use in, 18t, 19, 83
  large populations in, xiv, 7
  LPG use in, 18t, 19, 27, 83
  poverty reduction efforts and. See poverty and indoor air pollution
  socioeconomic profile, 14, 16–17

safety issues. See improved stoves programs; liquefied petroleum gas (LPG)
shared-use kitchens, 21, 22t, 23, 24t, 25–26

smoke. See indoor air pollution (IAP) and health
smuggling of LPG cylinders, 81, 86, 90
Social Investment Fund (FIS, Fondo de Inversión Social) and stoves improvement, 9, 40, 57
  See also improved stoves programs
  grants for, 55
  policy recommendations for, 99–100
  process of, 62–63
  purpose of FIS, 61
  reversion of household to open fire, 63
  stove design, 62f, 63, 70, 71–72
  subsidies, role of, 64, 76
socioeconomic profile issues in studies, 14, 15t, 16–17
Spain's financing of improved stoves project. See Intervida program
stoves. See improved stoves programs; planchas (wood-burning stoves with chimneys)
subsidies for improved stoves programs, 63–64, 64t, 74, 76, 78–79

technical improvements, xviii, 2, 9, 96–97
  See also improved stoves programs
technical unit to certify stoves, xix, 78–79
telephone coverage, 16
Tezulutlán stove project, 57, 58–59, 59f, 62, 63, 70–71
  See also improved stoves programs
tobacco. See environmental tobacco smoke (ETS)

TOMZA (Tomás Zaragoza), 88
traditional fuel use, high levels of,
      xiv, 7, 27, 93

urban communities
   fuels used for cooking, 17, 18*t*,
      19, 27, 82
   See also specific types of fuel
   kitchen exposure in, 21, 22*t*
   socioeconomic profile, 16
U.S. National Institutes of
      Health intervention study,
      6–7, 9

ventilation issues. *See* chimneys;
      indoor air pollution (IAP)
      and health

women's exposure to indoor air
      pollution

cooking smoke exposure, 1–2,
      21, 29
heart disease, 29
lung cancer, 29
open fires vs. *planchas* and, 4
poverty reduction efforts and, 8
role of women's groups to effect
      change, 96, 100
wood. *See* fuelwood
wood-burning stoves with chim-
      neys. *See planchas*
World Bank's Environmental
      Strategy for Energy Sector
      estimates, 1–2
World Health Organization
      (WHO) study on exposure
      to biomass smoke, xiii, 1,
      4, 35

ZETA (Miguel Zaragoza), 88